FOUL DEEDS AND SUSPICIOUS DEATHS IN AND AROUND CHESTERFIELD

Foul Deeds and Suspicious Deaths In & Around
CHESTERFIELD

GEOFFREY SADLER

Series Editor
Brian Elliott

Wharncliffe Books

First Published in 2003 by
Wharncliffe Books
an imprint of
**Pen and Sword Books Limited,
47 Church Street, Barnsley,
South Yorkshire. S70 2AS**

*For up-to-date information on other titles produced under the
Wharncliffe imprint, please telephone or write to:*

> **Wharncliffe Books
> FREEPOST
> 47 Church Street
> Barnsley
> South Yorkshire S70 2BR
> Telephone (24 hours): 01226 734555**

ISBN: 1-903425-30-1

A CIP catalogue record of this book is available from the
British Library

Cover illustration: *Front* – Moonlit scene; the church from Tapton Lane by Harry Ryde. *Chesterfield Local Studies Library*
Rear – Church of St Mary's and All Saints, Chesterfield.

Printed in the United Kingdom by
CPI UK

Contents

Introduction

'We didn't use to have violence in those days.'

It is a statement we have all become familiar with by now, the resigned comment delivered with a sad shake of the head by some senior citizen friend or colleague, harking back to a bygone paradise and convinced that present-day society is on its way to Armageddon. Nowadays it is often all too easy to agree with them as we hear of neighbours and relatives having their houses burgled, their cars stolen and trashed, and old folk afraid to venture on to streets roamed by violent gangs or 'druggies' out for a fix. And if these problems pass us by, television and the newspapers are always ready to regale us with horror stories of unfortunates battered and tortured in their homes by sadistic psychopaths, or children abducted and murdered by paedophile killers. We are right to be appalled at all of these crimes, but that is no excuse for pretending they never happened before. Believe me, they did. Violence is deplorable, but it is nothing new.

Turn to the newspapers of previous ages, or read back into the history books for even earlier centuries, and the similarities are startling. People in the fifteenth, eighteenth and nineteenth centuries were convinced they lived at the height of an unprecedented crime wave, in an age where the country was 'going to the dogs', and where 'something had to be done' to prevent total anarchy. I shall never forget reading through the pages of the *Derbyshire Times* and *Derbyshire Courier* issues for the 1850s and '60s, and being genuinely shocked to encounter case after case of crimes we tend to regard as modern aberrations. Child abduction and abuse, domestic violence, gang rapes, garottings, suicides and murders featured regularly in these pages. Read the *Derby Mercury* from 1732 onwards, and the story is much the same.

Chesterfield is the second largest town in Derbyshire, and the largest in the north of the county. A thriving, attractive market town surrounded by scenic landscapes, it presents a pleasant face to visitors, but a study of its past reveals that it has often been a dangerous place to live in. From medieval times to our own day Chesterfield and its neighbouring towns and villages have seen desperate encounters and shocking crimes, with suicides and brutal murders that have frequently achieved country-wide notoriety.

This book explores the darker side of Chesterfield and its outlying areas, shedding light on a catalogue of crimes, some of them relatively little known, others still claiming media attention. From the double murder at Chesterfield's parish church on 1 January 1434 we follow a blood-stained path that takes in the multiple executions at Tapton Bridge, and the savage punishment meted out to the members of the Babington plot and the 1817 'Pentrich Revolution'. The reader is witness to the murder of the luckless runaway couple at Winnats Pass in 1758, the fate of the victim of Derbyshire's last gibbet in 1815, and stands with 'gallant superintendent' Dennis Gorman in his vicious hand-to-hand battle with the Sothall sheep-stealer in 1870. The bloody thread of violence runs on to the grim Victorian yards and alleys of central Chesterfield, with their batterings, poisonings and razor murders.

I have been fortunate to have worked for the last seventeen years in the Chesterfield Local Studies Library, and to have access to its considerable resources. The library holds microfilm copies of the *Derby Mercury, Derbyshire Courier* and *Derbyshire Times,* together with a substantial file of cuttings from the *Sheffield Star,* which between them cover a period from 1732 to the present day. These newspapers report on crimes and police investigations, often with detailed accounts of trials and, from the mid-nineteenth century onward, the findings of coroners' inquests, where the causes of death are more thoroughly explored. They have provided me with the basic tools for my research. Standard works on crime and punishment in Derbyshire in the library stock have also provided valuable information, among them accounts of the trial of Antony Babington and of the Pentrich defendants, 'Annals of Crime in the Midland Circuit', and 'The Complete Book of Emigrants in Bondage', which lists persons transported to the American colonies prior to 1776, and gives instructive details of their offences; I have also found useful facts in periodicals such as the *Derbyshire Life & Countryside* and *Reflections* magazine.

I would like to express my thanks to my colleagues in the Chesterfield Local Studies Library and County Local Studies Library, Matlock, to Derbyshire Library Service for use of their images, to Philip Cousins for the kind loan of information and to the Ordnance Survey for permission to reproduce Old County Series maps. Special thanks must go to my good friend Dennis Middleton, who has toured virtually all of north Derbyshire with me to take the excellent photographs shown in the text, to Brian Davis for reproduction of the cover illustration, to Alun Waterhouse for his continued help in negotiating the new technology, and to Ann Krawszik and Sue Crabbe for the kind loan of additional photographs. Finally my thanks go to Brian Elliott and Wharncliffe Books for inviting me to take part in this project, and for their help and advice in making it happen.

Sources

1. Copies of local newspapers including the *Derbyshire Times*, the *Derbyshire Courier*, the *Derby Mercury*, and the *Sheffield Star*.
2. Anon. *Annals of Crime in the Midland Circuit*, 1859.
3. Christian, Roy. 'The Last of the Peasants' Revolts', 8 June 1967, *Country Life*.
4. Coldham, Peter Wilson. *The Complete Book of Emigrants in Bondage 1614-1775*, 1988.
5. Cooper, William Durrant. 'Notices of Anthony Babington of Dethick and of the Conspiracy of 1586', *Reliquary* Vol 2, 1861-62.
6. Large, J A. *Stories of the Derbyshire Dales*, 1997.
7. Pentrich Historical Society. *Pentrich Revolution Trail*, 2000.
8. Sitwell, Sir George. *The Story of the Sitwells*, unpublished galleys in Chesterfield Local Studies Library.
9. *Society for the Prosecution of Felons, 1744*. Photographic copy of original document in Chesterfield Local Studies Library.
10. Taylor, Philip. *May the Lord have mercy on your soul: murder and serious crime in Derbyshire 1732-1882*, 1989.
11. *The Trials of Jeremiah Brandreth, William Turner, Isaac Ludlam, George Weightman and others for High Treason, Under a Special Commission at Derby*, 1817.
12. Wood, Thomas Philpot. *T P Wood's Almanac*, 1868-1963.

Chapter 1

Murder at St Mary's
1434

When the Derbyshire landowner Sir Henry Pierrepoint rode into Chesterfield with his friends and servants to attend Mass on the morning of Friday 1 January 1434, the day must have seemed like any other. The party were familiar with the town and its inhabitants, and used to attending the church services on a regular basis. As they made their way along Saint Mary's Gate to the parish church of St Mary and All Saints, they could scarcely have failed to be impressed by the recently completed spire that reached two hundred feet high above them; only in later years would it achieve fame as the 'Crooked Spire' as its green timbers twisted to the force of lead and sunlight. Certainly it presented no threat to its visitors, who entered the building still suspecting nothing untoward. How

View of St Mary's church from Church Way. The spire would have been a familiar landmark when Henry Pierrepoint and his friends rode to Mass in January 1434.
Dennis Middleton

could they have known that soon they would be the victims of a murderous attack from which few of them would escape unscathed, and where two at least would pay with their lives.

In the early years of the fifteenth century, Derbyshire, like England itself, was a dangerous place to be, and not too much was going right. With the Hundred Years War against France now clearly lost, the nation lacked territory and prestige, and since the downfall of Richard II the kings who followed had struggled to keep a hold on the crown, beating off rebellious nobles only by a supreme effort. The massive wool boom of the previous century had generated great wealth for some, but with it had come widespread corruption by officials and the medieval equivalent of multi-national corporations. The resentment of the downtrodden lower orders, who stayed poor and oppressed as before, had exploded into the Peasants' Revolt of 1388, and although rebellion had been brutally crushed, the hatred smouldered on. Hardly surprising that law and order had broken down, and the country was beset by gangs of robbers – several of them renegade noblemen and their followers – who roamed their chosen 'turf' stealing and murdering as they pleased. The 'rymes of Robin Hood', whether of Sherwood or Barnesdale, were already familiar to most, and give a fair indication of the lawless state of late medieval society. In 1434, with the pious but ineffectual Henry VI on the throne, rival factions were already gearing up for the conflict which was later to be known as the Wars of the Roses, and several were eager to seize the chance to settle old scores.

Chesterfield, according to Sir George Sitwell in his unpublished work *The Story of the Sitwells*, 'was already notorious as a centre of disturbances, in which inhabitants of the same place and even members of the same family took up arms against each other', and this Friday morning in 1434 was to prove no exception. As Pierrepoint and his companions entered the church, a much larger body of men arrived in the town, two hundred strong, all of them heavily armed and encased in full body armour. They were led by Thomas Foljambe, the main local landowner and the sworn enemy of Pierrepoint, with whom he was determined to settle accounts. Based at Walton, a neighbouring parish to the south-west of the town, the

Foljambes were the lords of the manor of Chesterfield; the family had been major figures in North Derbyshire since Domesday, and would continue to loom large as High Sheriffs of the county into Tudor times. The group Thomas Foljambe led towards the church was drawn not only from his immediate retinue but from the Peak District further west, and included Richard Foljambe of Bonsall and the chaplain Thomas Cokke of Bakewell. These, and others, would later join the Lancastrian party in the Wars of the Roses, while Pierrepoint and company might fairly be described as Yorkists.

This was no spur of the moment action, however. Foljambe's plans had already been carefully laid. They involved Chesterfield's parish clerk, Thomas Mogynton, whose collusion was essential to the plot. Mogynton, who strikes one as a thoroughly nasty piece of work, was already inside the church, and went about his treacherous business, shutting the doors of the vestry, belfry and crucifix chamber to prevent any of the victims from hiding there. He then rang the church bells as a signal for the attack. Leaving roughly half his small army to guard the doors outside, barring entry with swords and battle-axes, Thomas Foljambe led a hundred men into the church, swords drawn as they sought their prey. As they approached the altar the vicar, Richard Dawson, met them, carrying the Eucharist. Showing considerable bravery, he tried to persuade them to leave, but was ordered to go back to the altar or die. As he retreated, and the other parishioners watched in horror, Foljambe's band broke their way in through the chancel door, to find Pierrepoint, the esquire Henry Longford, William Bradshaw and Thomas Hasilby standing to hear the Mass. At once the butchery began.

Pierrepoint's right hand was hacked with a sword, the force of the blow cutting through the thumb and first two fingers and putting him out of the fight. Hasilby's thumb was also severed, so that he too was left maimed and unable to draw a sword, even had he been armed. In the mayhem that ensued arrows were shot wildly over the altar, causing Dawson the vicar to throw down the Eucharist he held. One arrow hit and wounded the luckless Pierrepoint, already pouring blood from his injured hand. Now his five servants were set upon, and all were so badly

Vestry door, no doubt one of several closed by Thomas Mogynton before the Foljambes launched their attack. Dennis Middleton

hacked about 'that their lives were despaired of.'

Worse was to come for Longford and Bradshaw, who now became the targets for a hundred swords. Longford's death-blow was a vicious cut into the back of his leg 'behind the shin bones', which must have severed an artery. He fell to the ground and bled to death on the stone floor of the church. Bradshaw succumbed to a flurry of sword slashes aimed at his head, and 'the blood and brain sprang forth into the earth near a certain altar of the Blessed Mary and the same William Bradshaw died in the same church. And so the aforesaid evildoers most wickedly polluted the said church of God by their nefarious doings.'

Nor were they satisfied with the carnage they had caused. Henry Pierrepoint, weak and sickened from loss of blood, and doubtless thinking his last hour had come, was dragged from the church and away to the end of town, where an argument ensued as to what should be done with him. One man, William Brampton, yelled for him to be killed like the others, but at this stage some of the group were having second thoughts. Richard Foljambe of Bonsall and one Thomas Milne argued for his life to be spared, as awareness of the enormity of their crime dawned on them. Their plea was accepted, and Pierrepoint was sent home 'bleeding and maimed'. One assumes that Hasilby made a similar exit.

The murderous gang left town, hiding out at Holmesfield some miles to the north and waiting for the clamour to die down. At the Derby sessions in February a jury was called to inquire into the murders, but once more Foljambe had things organised. He employed Richard Brown, a shyster lawyer who presented the jury with a false list of the killers, 'containing the names of divers persons who never existed', and claiming on oath this was the list he had been given by the judges. The jury, though, were having none of it. Finding the list was a fraud, they agreed a verdict of murder against 'Thomas Foljambe of Walton, gentleman, and others'. Brown, however, had another trick up his sleeve, and added the word 'junior' after 'Foljambe', so the indictment now accused Foljambe's ten-year-old son, who obviously could not be held accountable. These and other shenanigans ensured that the killers remained free. Ten years later Thomas Foljambe, the instigator of the whole affair, was still in Chesterfield, where he held a high position in the Guild of the Blessed Mary. His victim, Sir Henry Pierrepoint, was also still there, as Alderman of the Guild of the Holy Cross. No doubt the latter harboured bitter thoughts when his wounds played up in the cold weather!

The last act, though, was yet to come. In September 1454, fully twenty years after their terrible crime, the killers were finally indicted. Many had already died, but the survivors numbered ninety or more, of whom thirteen were Chesterfield men. By a supreme irony Sir Henry Pierrepoint was a member of the grand jury which committed the offenders to the Marshalsea prison to await their trial. What happened after that seems not to have been recorded, but one suspects that it gave Sir Henry a certain amount of satisfaction.

Viewed across the succeeding centuries, this earliest of Chesterfield crimes remains perhaps the most shocking of all. Armed men, one of them a clergyman, breaking into a church and acting in collusion with another church official, threatening the vicar with death, maiming and murdering unarmed victims inside God's house in full view of the helpless parishioners. Judged by any standard, it was a horrific and brutal attack, and one that leaves an unpleasant taste in the mouth of the reader. Tourists visiting Chesterfield today are attracted by the church with its distinctive crooked spire, which has come to represent the town itself, but surely few of them know the terrible events of 1 January 1434, when murder came to St Mary's.

Chapter 2

'To Have Taken Away Her Majesties Lief' 1586

Twelve miles or so south-west of Chesterfield is the hamlet of Dethick, a small cluster of fields and three farmhouses surrounding the church of St John the Baptist. Virtually unchanged from Tudor times, the hamlet presents an idyllic rural vision that seems a world away from plotting and violence, yet it was here that plans were laid by a Derbyshire gentleman to kidnap and murder a queen.

Dethick was the home of Anthony Babington, who was born there in 1561 to a long-established family of local landowners. His ancestors had intermarried with several of Derbyshire's leading families, and held claim to land not only in the county but also in Nottinghamshire and other parts of England. One

Manor and Babington Farms, Dethick. Dennis Middleton

memorable account describes him as 'a yonge man, well featured, and of good proportion in all the lyneamentes of his bodie, of a most pregnante fyne witt and great capacitie, had a watchinge head, and a most proude aspiringe mynde'. In other words, handsome, witty, intelligent and charming. Anthony clearly had it all. Unfortunately, this description forms part of a posthumous record. For, although nowadays we would probably not consider him a hardened wrongdoer, Anthony Babington lived in the Elizabethan age, and his own time judged him guilty of the most heinous crime of treason.

Anthony was still a child when his father died, and he inherited the family estates. Not long afterwards his mother remarried, and interestingly enough the new stepfather was Henry Foljambe, some of whose relatives we have already met. A gentler man than his medieval forbears, Henry proved a kind and generous parent, and Anthony remembered his upbringing and that of his brothers with gratitude. The Babingtons were staunch Roman Catholics, and Anthony was raised in the faith

Church of St John the Baptist, Dethick, the family church of the Babingtons, who enlarged and improved the building around 1530. Dennis Middleton

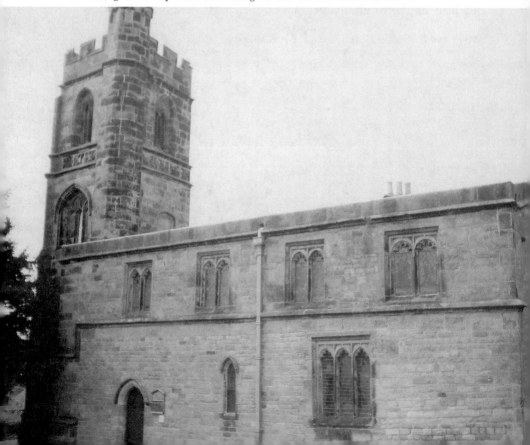

of his fathers, from which he never swerved. It was his bad luck that Elizabeth I, a Protestant queen, was on the throne, and that these were days of persecution for English Catholic believers, the pendulum having swung violently back from the recent burnings of Protestants during the reign of Elizabeth's late half-sister, 'Bloody Mary'.

While still a youngster, Anthony met another queen. Chatsworth House was not far from Dethick, and there Mary, Queen of Scots was held under virtual 'house arrest' in the care of George, Earl of Shrewsbury and his formidable countess, Bess of Hardwick. As a boy, Anthony Babington was sent to Hardwick to serve as a page with Shrewsbury, and would undoubtedly have seen the captive monarch at close quarters. Shrewsbury regarded his job as gaoler as a thankless task, but the young Anthony would seem to have been impressed by the beauty and dignified bearing of this imprisoned queen whose beliefs he shared, and it is likely he developed a schoolboy 'crush' at an early stage. With this admiration, which was never to leave him for the remainder of his life, there grew an abiding hatred of the Protestant Elizabeth, a heretic ruler who presided over the judicial murder of his co-religionists. Already the first sparks were flaring, which in time would fuel the flames of treason.

Worship of Mary as an unattainable ideal, plus the religious fervour of his personal beliefs, was to prove a potent and dangerous mixture. That it was still in the mind of Anthony Babington through his studies at Lincoln's Inn, and on his return to Dethick as a country gentleman in his twenties, is evident enough. In the fateful year of 1586, he travelled to France, where in Paris he quickly made the acquaintance of several fellow-Catholics who, like himself, were eager to see Elizabeth ousted and Mary set to rule in her place. These new companions included Thomas Morgan, a former employee of the Earl of Shrewsbury. Others in the entourage were Charles Paget, John Savage, and two Catholic priests, Ballard and Gilbert Gifford. Together they determined on a plan to liberate Mary from her captivity, kidnap and murder Elizabeth, and set a Catholic queen on the throne.

On returning to England, Anthony moved between Dethick

and London seeking new recruits, meeting his co-conspirators and pushing ahead with his murderous plan. Sadly for him, he and the other plotters were out of their depth. Elizabeth was well served by Europe's most ruthlessly efficient intelligence service, headed by Sir Francis Walsingham. The latter had already infiltrated Anthony's 'cell' through Gifford, who was acting as a double agent, and knew everything about the plotters and their aims. Unaware that they were under surveillance, the plotters made an arrangement with a brewer from Burton-on-Trent to provide special casks of beer to be sent to Mary's household at Chartley Hall in Staffordshire. Each cask had a false bottom which contained a small box for the use of secret messages, and weekly deliveries at Chartley were taken by a sympathetic butler, who then handed on the box and its contents to Mary's secretary. Mary's reply would follow, in the same cask, the following week. The only problem was that the plan had been set up by Gifford in order to trap the conspirators, and he had bribed the brewer, who was also 'in the know'. The messages sent in the casks were intercepted en route, and their codes quickly broken by Walsingham's spies.

In July 1586 Mary was foolish enough to reply to one of these letters, using the same beer-barrel route, and this prompted a suicidally indiscreet response from Babington himself. Anthony held out the unlikely vision of an invasion from Catholic Europe, a mass uprising of the English Catholic population, and Mary's own liberation. Worst of all, he envisaged the death of Elizabeth. To a staunch Catholic like himself, this would have seemed perfectly justified. In a Protestant land that saw itself under threat from Catholic neighbours, it was treason of the foulest kind. His impassioned outpourings now drew Mary herself into the spymaster's net. Replying on 17 July, she worded her answer more cautiously, but made no comment on the proposed assassination of Elizabeth. This apparent approval of the murder of a fellow monarch was to prove a fatal mistake for her. Having had sight and knowledge of all their correspondence, Walsingham decided to move in for the kill.

It was at Dethick that he struck first. Ballard, the priest, was staying there while Babington was in London, and Walsingham had him arrested. Babington tried to set up the kidnapping and assassination of Elizabeth with Savage and another plotter, Charnock, but the plan fell through. Soon afterwards he and his friends found themselves having to answer awkward questions put by the authorities, and sensed that they were under suspicion. Their regular haunts were no longer safe, and they fled for their lives. Pursued as fugitives, they were reduced to hiding in woods and amateurish attempts at disguising themselves failed to save them. On 14 August 1586 Anthony and the others were arrested and brought to London, the capital erupting in celebration of the thwarting of their dastardly plot on the life of the queen. Not long afterwards, Mary, Queen of Scots was also arrested on the same charge of treason, and would later die on the headsman's block.

Following a full confession probably obtained under torture, Anthony Babington and his companions were found guilty of 'conspiracy for the invasion of the realme to assist the Invadors, for the deliverye and setting upp of the Scottish Quene, and for surprising the Royall person of oure soveraigne Ladie the Queen's Majesty, and allso to have taken away her Majesties lief.' All were sentenced to death. Anthony himself was only twenty-five years old, and a fellow plotter Chidiock Tichborne - one of his own recruits- was also in his twenties. It was Tichborne who, on the eve of his execution, wrote the moving poem which perhaps stands as the most fitting epitaph to these deluded, idealistic young men whose lives would so soon be cut short:

> *I sought my death, and found it in the womb*
> *I looked for life, and saw it was a shade*
> *I trod this earth, and knew it was my tomb*
> *And now I die, and now I was but made*
> *The glass is full, and now the glass is run*
> *And now I live, and now my life is done.*

The first of the plotters were brought to execution on 13 September 1586. Ironically the place chosen was near Lincoln's Inn fields, where Anthony had studied not long before and which he now revisited for the last time. Elizabeth was determined to make an example of them, and the manner of their death was terrible. Each man was hanged and cut down while still breathing, then castrated, gutted and disembowelled, the

Manor Farm, Dethick, boyhood home of Anthony Babington. Dennis Middleton

internal organs taken out and burnt in front of the suffering victim. Anthony Babington looked on as Ballard and Savage were put to death, while his companions turned away, unable to watch. Then, one by one, they died. In his final agony, Anthony is said to have cried 'Have mercy on me, Lord Jesus'. Fittingly, he spoke the words in Latin. Once life was extinct, the corpses were hacked into quarters and set on spikes, together with their severed heads, as a warning to would-be traitors.

The Babington plot was over, and with it the life of the young man who lent it his name. Today, the hamlet where he grew to manhood shows few indications of those desperate days, but perhaps the ghost of Anthony Babington still walks the country lanes, dreaming vainly of what might have been.

Chapter 3

Of Six and Twelve
1637–79

With the death of Elizabeth I, and the crowning of her nephew and the son of her rival Mary, Queen of Scots as James I, the relative stability of the Tudor period gave way to the nervous decades leading up to the Civil Wars. Short of money, under pressure from a rising mercantile puritan parliament and dogged by lack of military and diplomatic success at home and abroad, the monarchy floundered from one crisis to the next. Witchcraft trials and the narrowly thwarted Gunpowder Plot proved to be omens of worse to come. By the late 1630s, the country was divided against itself and heading for war. In such an unstable climate, it was only natural that crime and criminals should flourish.

That Chesterfield, a thriving market town and the centre for North Derbyshire's trade and commerce, was not immune is plain from the cryptic note in T P Wood's *Almanac* on the year 1637. Quoting from earlier sources, it states: 'On 16 March the Assizes were held at Chesterfield, and five men and one woman were hanged at Tapton Bridge.'

Tapton Bridge spanned the River Rother on the north-eastern outskirts of Chesterfield, and evidently this is where the gallows must have stood. That the Assizes were held in the town at this time was unusual. This court dealt only with the most serious of offences that were, as in this case, a hanging matter. As a rule, Chesterfield, whose House of Correction in its damp, unhealthy location to the south of the borough was built only to house short-term offenders, tried only the minor or middling crimes, referring the murderers, traitors and rapists to the Assizes at Derby. On this occasion Chesterfield was chosen due to a severe outbreak of plague at Derby, which prevented the trials taking place there.

One wonders what were the crimes of the men and the woman whose corpses hung from the gallows on that day. Were theirs separate offences, or were they guilty of a collective act? And what terrible deed condemned them to this end? Even in those pitiless days, theirs must have been a serious offence. The records keep silence, and the reason is still a mystery today. All we know for certain is that they met a slow and painful death, strangling in the hempen nooses, dangling above the river in plain sight of the Chesterfield townsfolk, who no doubt turned out after the fashion of the day for an hour or so of grim public entertainment. Like Stuart crime, Stuart punishment was notable for its brutality.

The Civil Wars of the 1640s left bitter, long-lasting hatreds that often divided members of the same family for years to come. They also added considerably to the criminal classes by the disbandment of regiments once the fighting was over. Hundreds of potentially violent men were turned loose to fend for themselves across the country, or starve. A more effective recipe for the spread of violent crime can scarcely be imagined. Desperate, skilled in the use of weaponry and the tactics of ambush, these unemployed ex-servicemen proved to be the most dangerous of criminals, and were often the hardest to catch. Former cavalry troopers served as precursors of the later highwaymen, while ex-footsoldiers were role models of the footpad. Both preyed ruthlessly on helpless travellers, robbing them of their valuables and goods, and sometimes of their lives.

Foremost of Derbyshire's outlaws in the Stuart age were the band of desperadoes better known as 'the Bracy gang', described in August 1679 at the trial in Derby of 'Twelve Notorious Highway Men, Murderers, and Clippers of Money'. This group of robbers was headed by a certain 'Mr Bracy' who led his followers in a brief but violent rampage across the East Midlands during the 1670s. While their favoured locations lay away from North Derbyshire, in Derby, Nottingham and Newark, one of their most audacious robberies was made at the village of Morton in the north of the county, where the gang broke into the house of Captain John Munday, Esquire under cover of darkness. Munday and his family were overpowered and bound tightly in their beds. Threatened with violence and torture by their captors, they revealed where their valuables

Sitwell Arms, *Morton, the village where the Bracy gang struck to rob Captain Munday in 1679.* Ann Krawszik

were hidden, and the gang made off in triumph with a staggering haul of £1,200 in gold, silver and plate. Two months later, obviously having sized up their victim, they robbed a waggon loaded with barrels of coin in neighbouring Nottinghamshire, and this time topped their previous figure with 'takings' of £1,800!

One gang member was captured at Ockbrook in south Derbyshire soon after, and as pursuit of the fugitives intensified most of the band were rounded up. Two of the gang, Richard Piggen and John Baker, managed to escape the gallows and were pardoned, the former having turned King's evidence to inform on his luckless colleagues. 'Mr Bracy' also escaped hanging, but his end was less pleasant. Hurrying to visit his dying wife at an inn close to Nottingham, he was found and cornered by a sheriff's posse. In true Wild West style Bracy was handed a horse by his son, and rode for his life. Unfortunately his mount balked at the fence that barred his way to freedom, and shots from the pursuing lawmen killed the horse and wounded Bracy. In a shoot-out reminiscent of 'Butch Cassidy and the Sundance Kid' the Stuart gang-boss fought on until he sustained a fatal wound. Collapsing, he was borne back to the inn, where he breathed his last.

The Tapton Bridge hangings, and the career of the Bracy gang, are merely the most striking examples of what must have been a much more widespread lawlessness and violence. For every Morton robbery there would have been scores of lesser thefts from unwary travellers, and the mass execution outside Chesterfield must have been greatly outnumbered by the hangings of individual criminals. What is beyond dispute is that the instability of the Stuart period led to an upsurge in crime, and the dawn of the age of the highwayman. As the eighteenth century approached, the problem remained unsolved, and was set to grow still worse.

Chesterfield and North Derbyshire would be no exception to the rule.

Chapter 4

'Many and Frequent Felonys'
1700s

In the eighteenth century Derbyshire, and with it the rest of England, changed. The innovations of the Agricultural and Industrial Revolutions transformed the countryside and saw a mass exodus to the rapidly growing towns and cities. As the nation made the change from a rural to an urban society and the population boomed, these years echoed the fifteenth century as a time of great prosperity for the favoured few. Plantation slavery swelled the coffers of the 'plantocracy', while early speculators made their 'killings' in the City of London. The problem for the country's rich, however, was the lack of law enforcement agencies to help them hang on to their wealth and keep it out of the clutches of an increasingly discontented population, who as usual remained poor and envious of the 'fat cats' above them. Uprisings of disaffected farm labourers and factory hands were matched by highway robbery, which now reached its peak. Whether attacked by the humble footpad or the more glamorous mounted highwayman, wealthy travellers ran a high risk of losing money and property, and rapes and murders on the road were not unknown. Meanwhile the example of the Bracy gang a century before showed clearly that no Derbyshire gentleman could feel safe inside his own house if there were rich pickings for desperate men.

It was evident to Derbyshire's gentry that they were faced with a terrifying new crime wave, for which they had no answer at all. Worse still, they knew that the criminals often had the sympathy of the honest poor, who regarded the making of fortunes while others starved as a kind of theft, and viewed highwaymen and robbers in the same heroic light as Robin Hood in medieval times. Like the legendary outlaw, it was felt, the highwayman robbed the rich and gave to the poor, even if the 'poor' were the

WHEREAS: many and frequent felonys in stealing of (goods?) and sheep have been lat
committed in and about the town and in the parish of Chesterfield in the county of Derby. The goo
and chattells of Us, whose names are hereunder written, or of some, or one of Us, And in order
prevent if possible the like evil practices for the future, and for and toward the raising of a fu
sufficient for the Rewarding of any persons or persons who shall make discovery of the offender
effenders herin. It is covenanted and confirmed and fully agreed and by and amongst us whe
hands are herunto put and seals are fixed and each of us for himself and herself singly, severa
and separately and for his and her several and respective (?) and not jointly one for another or
the (?). one of another doth mutually covenant promise and agree each to and with the other th
at all or any time or times for and during the term of 7 years, to be reckoned and computed fr
the day of the date of these presents. When any such felony or felonys as aforesaid shall be done
committed, well and truly to pay into the hands of Gervase Gardiner Gentleman, John Fisher butc
and Samuel Earnshaw butcher all of Chesterfield aforesaid upon demand, the several su
herunder written and set against our respective names for and as a stock or fund for the encourag
and rewarding therout of any person or persons who shall discover any such said offendor
offendors. So he, she or they may be prosecuted to conviction and we whose names are herun
written and seals affixed aforesaid do also hereby jointly and severally authorise direct impor
them the said Gervase Gardiner, John Fisher and Samuel Earnshaw upon any such felons
felonys as aforesaid being done or committed and to promise such reward or rewards for
discovering of the offendors therin. As they shall think proper .... the Sum of twenty pou
for any one felony and upon their conviction as aforesaid to pay the same to the persons institut
thereto out of the same beforementioned stock or fund. In Witness whereof we have respectiv
herunto put our hands and seals the Twenty Eighth day of March in the Year of our Lord C
Thousand Seven...hundred and ffourty ffour. Society for the Prosecution of Felons; doc, 28 March 17

robbers themselves!

The property-owners of the nation responded with a harsher set of laws and punishments, most of them aimed at crimes against property. The death penalty was extended to a massive 200 offences, four times as many as the previous century, and this 'Bloody Code' as it was known, was ferociously implemented. Unfortunately it failed to halt the crime wave, which continued unabated. Catching the criminals was the main problem, and in an attempt to achieve this local gentry and tradesmen combined to form Societies for the Prosecution of Felons, putting up reward money for information on criminals, or their capture. It has been claimed that the practice began in Yorkshire in the 1750s, but in fact such a Society was set up in Chesterfield as early as 28 March 1744, and a copy and transcript of the original document are held in Chesterfield Local Studies Library.

Explaining that 'many and frequent felonys in stealing of goods and sheep have been lately committed in and about the town and in the parish of Chesterfield in the county of Derby', the signatories agreed to pay 'into the hands of Gervase Gardiner Gentleman, John Fisher butcher and Samuel Earnshaw butcher all of Chesterfield aforesaid' the sum set against each name, sufficient to provide a reward of £20 for 'the discovering of the offendors therin.' Several leading townsmen such as Joshua Jebb and George Milnes were among those who signed. Societies for the Prosecution of Felons continued in being through the nineteenth century, and a handful exist as social clubs to this day, but just like the increased death penalty offences, they failed to stamp out the problem.

Reporting on the Nottingham Assizes of 16 March 1780, the *Derby Mercury* notes several Derbyshire defendants charged with a variety of offences:

> *Benjamin Wykes, William Turner, and Joseph Archer, were indicted for stealing on the 3 February last, out of a common Stage travelling Cart, belonging to Samuel Tomlinson of Crich, as it was standing at Southwingfield in this county, 290lb of India Cotton, packed up in Bags....the Property of Messrs Arkwright, Need, and Strutt.. to be kept on hard labour for three years on the River Thames.*

> *Samuel Cotton, for stealing Joints of Pork from John Whawell's*
> *Shop at Repton, ordered to be privately whipped.*
>   *Elizabeth Bingham, indicted for the murder of her Female Child*
> *at Norton... was acquitted.*
>   *Henry Bacon, for stealing from John Cooper of Chesterfield a*
> *Pair of Shoes, a Pair of Silver Shoe Buckles, one Pair of*
> *Stockings, one Handkerchief, and a Parcel of Halfpence... ordered*
> *to be imprisoned for three Years in the House of Correction.*

Considering many were hanged for less than the above offences, some of those concerned got off fairly lightly. The acquittal of Elizabeth Bingham is especially interesting, and in fact one of the drawbacks of the 'Bloody Code' was that its severity often prompted a 'backlash' of acquittals by sympathetic judges and juries, not least when the defendant was a woman.

No such luck for the highwayman James Meadows, who appeared at the same Assizes charged with a violent robbery on the road near Ashbourne where he had made off with 'Thirty-seven Guineas in Gold, and three Shillings in Silver.' For Meadows, it was the death penalty: 'His Lordship gave him not the least Hopes of Life, but exhorted him to prepare to meet his Fate with a Christian Resignation; and then pronounced the dreadful Sentence; and we hear that he will be executed on Friday in Easter Week, the 31 Instant.' Alone of the defendants, Meadows ended his life on the Derby gallows.

Up until 1776, when the United States declared its independence, transportation to the American colonies provided judges with a useful alternative, and a number of Derbyshire offenders were sentenced to death only to be reprieved for shipment abroad. Coldham's epic work *The Complete Book of Emigrants in Bondage 1614-1775* lists the names of such locals as the pickpocket John Williams, sentenced in 1730, horsethieves Robert Ashmore (14 years) and Joseph Barker (7 years) in 1745 and 1772, and the sheepstealer George Bradway (14 years) in 1754. What became of them afterwards we are left to wonder, but one doubts that it was a pleasant experience.

All the same, it was surely preferable to the fate of Thomas Nevill, another Derbyshire highwayman, whose death in Derby in April 1795 was reported in the pages of the *Mercury:*

> *He looked upon his approaching dissolution with undaunted firmness and obstinate resolution. He was carried to execution in a mourning coach, attended by a hearse; where he assisted his executioner to fasten the rope to the tree, after which he drew his cap over his face and leaped from the cart into never ending eternity.*

Having remarked on Nevill's last act of courage, the reporter adds a wry and revealing footnote:

> *One would have thought the severe hand of justice would have operated as a terror to evil doers, but on the contrary several persons witnessing this awful scene had their pockets picked.*

There could be no better indictment of the ineffectiveness of the 'Bloody Code'. Even at the foot of the gallows, for Derbyshire's criminals it was 'business as usual.'

Chapter 5

Elopement to Death
1758

One morning in April in the year 1758 two riders drew rein before the *Royal Oak Inn* at Stoney Middleton, a Peakland village on the road to Castleton. Roused from his bed at what was an unusually early hour, the landlord greeted the pair. They proved to be a young couple who answered to the names of Allan and Clara, and whose accents identified them as hailing from north of the border, in Scotland. The landlord noted that the lady was very attractive, and that the young man's good looks were only slightly marred by a missing front tooth. He also did not fail to notice the remarkably fine clothes they both wore, and the heavily weighted saddlebag the gentleman carried. He arranged for the feeding and watering of their horses, and had a meal prepared for them, and while he was doing so was asked for directions to Peak Forest. No doubt the landlord smiled as they asked him. Now he knew why they were here.

The former Royal Oak Inn, *Stoney Middleton, where Allan and Clara halted on their last journey in 1758.* Dennis Middleton

The village of Peak Forest, destination of the runaway Scottish couple. Unfortunately it was never reached. Dennis Middleton

Peak Forest was a settlement that lay on the far side of Castleton, beyond the Winnats Pass. Due to some clerical oversight, its church and minister were not answerable to any bishop, which enabled the incumbent to provide marriage licences to all comers, describing them as 'foreign marriages'. This useful facility had already drawn many eloping couples to Peak Forest, which had now become Derbyshire's answer to

Peak Forest Church of King Charles the Martyr, the Gretna Green of Derbyshire, where, due to an administrative anomaly, the vicar was able to marry fugitive couples from outside the parish. Dennis Middleton

Gretna Green, and Allan and Clara were proof that news of the place had travelled as far as Scotland. Keeping his thoughts to himself, the landlord outlined the route through Castleton and the Winnats Pass to Peak Forest, and was thanked for his trouble.

Refreshed and rested, the couple rode on to Castleton, and once more halted at one of the inns in the town. This time, however, their rich apparel and weighty belongings drew the attention of a less well-intentioned group. Four lead-miners drinking at the inn saw rich pickings, and only two obstacles in their way to illicit wealth. Following the pair, they hid themselves in the Winnats Pass, a narrow gully flanked by looming walls of rock, and prepared their ambush.

Allan and Clara rode into the pass, and were promptly attacked and seized by the miners, who dragged them from their horses, and into a nearby barn. Both were quickly overpowered, and the young woman begged them to spare her life.

Winnats Pass, scene of the ambush where Allan and Clara were robbed and murdered. Dennis Middleton

For a moment her beauty caused them to hesitate, but not for long. The robbers knew that if either of their victims went free and the attack was reported, all four of them would end their lives on the gallows. The picks they carried for everyday use in the mine now proved to be murder weapons, and Allan and Clara died horribly as the blades were driven into their skulls. Stripped of their money and jewellery, and probably their fine clothes too, they lay lifeless as the miners used their picks to dig a makeshift grave, and buried the couple. The two horses were allowed to run off, the killers probably not wanting to draw attention to themselves by stealing the animals as well. Dividing their loot, the four men moved away in different directions from the scene of their crime.

Three or four days later, the horses were found wandering on the moors near Castleton, still wearing their saddles and bridles. The men who found them brought the animals into Castleton itself, and a search party set off to find the couple. The area around the village was scoured thoroughly, including a descent into the deep ravine of Eldon Hole, where it was thought the bodies might have been hidden, but no trace of the couple was found. The horses were positively identified as theirs by the landlord of the *Royal Oak* when they passed through the village en route to Chatsworth. The search having proved unavailing, the disappearance of the couple remained a mystery until ten years later, when a shaft was sunk at Winnats Pass, and two skeletons were found. They were the remains of a man and a woman, and the missing front tooth of the male skeleton served as proof that these were the bodies of Allan and Clara, who had obviously died in suspicious circumstances. No clues were found as to the identities of their killers, however, and after a while the excitement died down once again.

A further ten years on, the facts of the case were finally revealed. In his last hour of life, lead-miner James Ashton made a death-bed confession to the vicar of Castleton that he and three other men had committed the crime. He described the ambush at Winnats Pass, the plea of the beautiful young girl for her life, and the terrible nature of the killings. Apparently none of his fellow-criminals had benefited from their ill-gotten gains.

Clara's ornate morocco leather side-saddle, as displayed in the Speedwell Cavern Gift Shop. Dennis Middleton

One man had plunged to his death from a rocky height near to the pass, another had perished in a rock fall, while the third had gone out of his mind. Whether memory of the crime had any bearing on their eventual ends we may never know, but no doubt many would regard it as a kind of poetic justice.

Clara's ornate morocco leather side-saddle with its hand-stitched designs is still in existence, and may be viewed in its glass case in the Speedwell Cavern Gift Shop at the entrance to the Winnats Pass. It is now the sole memorial of the terrible crime that took place nearby, some two and a half centuries in the past.

Chapter 6

Saved By Her Skirts
1762

Only a few years after Allan and Clara met their deaths at Winnats Pass, the village of Stoney Middleton through which they had travelled was the scene for the most spectacular failed suicide bid in Derbyshire's history. The despairing leap of Hannah Baddaley, and her miraculous escape from death, are surely still unequalled to this day.

Hannah, a young unmarried girl living at Stoney Middleton, had attracted the romantic attentions of William Barnsley, a young fellow of her own age who was a native of the same village. Their courtship continued for some time, and appears to have reached an intensely passionate stage. At least, this was true of Hannah, but it seems that William's passion began to cool, and the romance came to an abrupt end. Rejected by her

Hannah Baddaley's Cottage, Stoney Middleton, home of Derbyshire's most famous failed suicide. Dennis Middleton

lover, Hannah was devastated, and decided that life was no longer worth living. As soon as possible, she would end it all, and what better way to cut short her life than to jump from the cliffs overlooking her home village. Who knows, perhaps William might be an unwilling witness to her death? No doubt Hannah felt it would be a lesson to him.

One morning in 1762 she left her home and climbed uphill away from the village until she stood at the edge of the grey limestone cliffs that loomed above the main road through Stoney Middleton. Scanning that sheer wall of rock, and the fifty foot drop to the road below, anyone else might well have faltered, but Hannah's mind was made up. Setting down her bonnet and gloves, she declaimed a prepared speech freeing William from any blame for her death, then launched herself into empty air in what she intended to be a final act of self-destruction.

Amazingly, Hannah did not die. The voluminous skirts and petticoats she was wearing billowed out as she leapt, effectively

Lover's Leap, Stoney Middleton, the cliff from which Hannah Baddaley threw herself in 1762, only to be saved by her billowing skirts. Dennis Middleton

acting as parachutes that slowed her fall. Even so, the downward plunge was terrible enough. The falling girl struck against rocks and thorny bushes, and was fortunate not to be killed by the impact. When she eventually struck the ground it was not on the road she landed, but in the softer earth of a sawpit at the foot of the cliff. There Hannah lost consciousness.

Horrified onlookers rushed to help her, and carried her bruised and bloody to her house. Slowly and painfully, she recovered, and once she had got over the shock she took up her life again. By now, though, William was no longer foremost in her mind. The terrible 'near-death experience' she had endured had put their relationship into perspective, and as far as Hannah was concerned he belonged to a long-dead past. Unfortunately, the story has a sad ending, for Hannah lived only a few years more. Whether due to her injuries, or other causes, she died in 1768 aged only twenty-six. Memory of her amazing suicide bid is kept alive by an account of the incident displayed on a board on the former inn at the base of the cliff, and the place itself, which has ever since borne the name of 'Lover's Leap'.

Chapter 7

He Could Not Expect Any Mercy
1786

Always one of the ugliest of crimes, rape is usually not a matter of mere sexual gratification, but a brutal, violent display of power and control over a victim unwilling, but too weak to resist. Still all too common today, there are times when it seems the crime is not punished as severely as it ought to be. In the Georgian era, itself a brutal age, one thing was certain for convicted rapists. All they could look forward to was the hangman's rope. And when the time came, some of them left this world in an unexpected fashion.

On Tuesday 8 August 1786, Corporal James Haliburton of the 5th Foot Regiment was brought to trial at the Derby Summer Assizes, charged with the rape of Millicent Smith, a farmer's wife, at the village of Biggin, south of Wirksworth. As a soldier, Haliburton's conduct had been beyond reproach, and one of his officers was only too eager to testify as to his good character. Unfortunately for him, and even more so for his luckless victim, he had behaved very differently to Mrs Smith, and the violence he had shown in committing the assault on her clearly horrified those who heard the evidence in the six-hour trial. Convicted and sentenced, Haliburton was told 'that he could not expect any mercy, as he had greatly aggravated the Crime by his Brutality', and had better 'make the best Use of his Time in preparing for another World'.

The guilty man evidently took this to heart. When the grim procession arrived at the place of execution at midday on 2 September, and Haliburton had been prayed over by Rev Mr Henry, he 'desired that a hymn might be sung'. The choice made was No 62 in a book of hymns by Isaac Watts, namely: *Come, let us join our cheerful songs/ With angels round the throne.* From a modern perspective, it's difficult not to see this as the ultimate

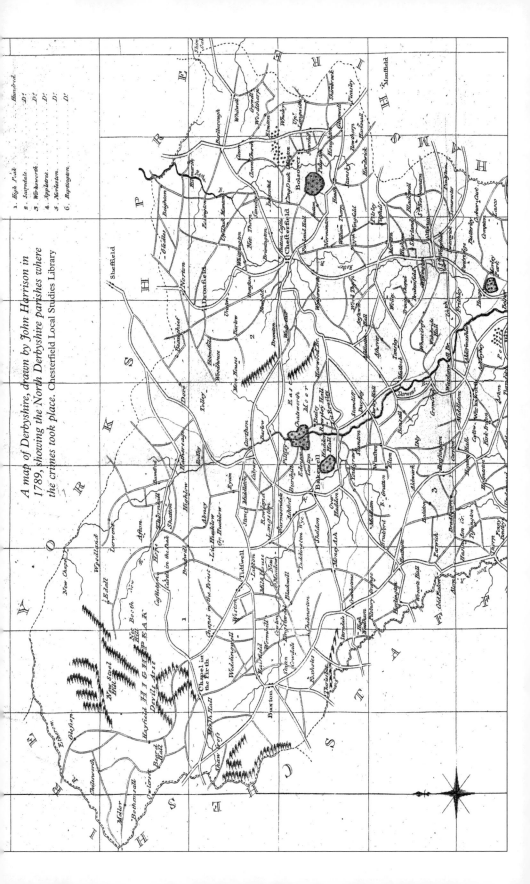

A map of Derbyshire, drawn by John Harrison in 1789, showing the North Derbyshire parishes where the crimes took place. Chesterfield Local Studies Library

in 'gallows humour', but apparently the condemned man joined in and 'sung with much fervour'! Prior to the cart being driven away from underneath him, he asked the onlookers to pray for him, and just before the rope took him off he is said to have uttered the words: 'For if God has not Mercy on my Soul I am eternally undone.'

In spite of this late religious conversion, a footnote in the report showed that the worst of human nature remained unchanged. At 2 pm that same day, another rape was committed at Ireton Wood by a hawker of lace.

Chapter 8

Theft, Self-Murder and the Gibbet 1801–15

As the nineteenth century dawned, Chesterfield and North Derbyshire once more found themselves a prey to criminal activity. On 14 August 1801 two highwaymen, George Lacy Powell and John Drummond, mounted the gallows at Derby together with three other offenders. Before their execution, they confessed to an unsolved crime, namely the murder of a Mr Hill on his return home from the market at Alfreton, a town some ten miles south of Chesterfield.

A few years later, on 31 August 1808, Chesterfield's annual races began on the track at Whittington Moor just north of the town itself. While most of the population were engrossed in the running of the horses, a band of thieves pulled off one of the most audacious robberies of the century, ransacking Chesterfield's famous parish church and escaping undetected. The official report by the vicar, parish clerk and churchwardens reveals some of the shock and outrage they must have felt at the time:

The first race day at night, some thieves picked the lock of the door opposite the clerk's house, went down the north aisle, picked that lock at the bottom, tried the chancel door, opposite, which was bolted inside; they then picked the other chancel door lock, and the vestry, four double locks on the chest padlocks, wrenched two clasp locks open, (which they could not pick) with the sexton's pick-axe, drank one bottle of wine, and took four with them; took the two silver cups, the large salver dish, and the small plate, and got clear off the same way; but left the two large flagons in the chest.

The value of the stolen items is not divulged, but what struck the outraged officials most, as it does the reader today, was the sheer daring, enterprise and skill in getting at the church's treasures. That the gang included a specialist pick-lock is

Parish Church of St James, Barlborough, the village where William Wells murdered George Bingham in 1803. Dennis Middleton

obvious, and the chances are they had at least some inside knowledge of where the valuables were to be found, but the use of the sexton's pick-axe when some locks defied them, and the impudent drinking of sacred wine before their departure shows how sure they were of themselves. It seems that their high opinion of their abilities was not misplaced, as the loot was never recovered and none of them was brought to justice!

On 17 March 1803 William Wells came to trial at Derby, charged with the murder of George Bingham at the village of Barlborough, to the east of Chesterfield. His victim was described as 'an old man upwards of seventy years of age', and it was evident that Wells would hang for his crime. His death, two days after the trial, was also harrowing. When the cart drove off to leave him hanging, the rope broke and he fell heavily to the ground, half-choked but still living. Having survived once, Wells' luck was at an end. The cart returned and he was strung up once again, this time with fatal results.

The same year of 1803 saw Chesterfield chosen as the temporary 'open prison' for a number of French officers taken prisoner in the Napoleonic Wars. These new visitors were allowed out on parole, and became quite well known to the town's inhabitants. Some were returned in prisoner exchanges, but many stayed until Napoleon's exile to Elba in 1814. Over the years, several officers married local ladies, and settled down, although there were a couple of escape bids.

The most bizarre event concerning the prisoners was a suicide by an unnamed officer, recounted in the *Star* newspaper of 1807. This man apparently stole £1,000 from a fellow-prisoner, Colonel Richemont, while the latter was staying at the *Falcon Inn* on Low Pavement. Such a large amount could not have been easy to hide, and once the theft was discovered, it was not long before the culprit was tracked down. It was the response of the guilty man that shocked his fellow prisoners and the whole town. Admitting his misdeed, he at once swallowed poison of some kind, and made certain he would not survive by grabbing a knife and plunging it into his own breast. He lived for only a short time after. He had cheated the hangman, but in those days suicide - or, as the coroner's jury described it in their verdict, 'self-murder' – was regarded as a

Falcon Inn, *Low Pavement, now the offices of the Barnsley Building Society, the scene of the bizarre suicide of a French prisoner of war in 1807.* Dennis Middleton

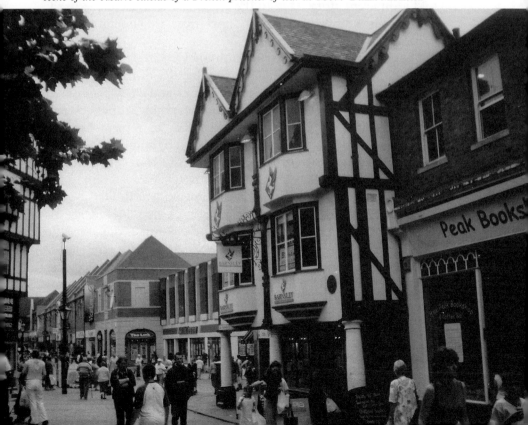

grave sin, and one that meant he could not be buried in consecrated ground. Instead, the unfortunate man was carried one night to a cross-roads, and was secretly buried there. Neither his name, nor that of his burial-place, was revealed in the account. As a final, sinister detail, a stake was driven into his side before the earth was shovelled over him. Evidently those who were burying him still believed in vampires, and the wandering of unquiet spirits.

Perhaps a dozen miles north-west of Chesterfield, just beyond Stoney Middleton in the vicinity of Tideswell, lies the bleak area of moorland known as Wardlow Mires. Here, in the year 1815, when Napoleon met his final defeat, another macabre event took place. Hannah Oliver, an elderly widow of seventy years, was the keeper of the toll-bar cottage giving access to the western turnpike road, the same road travelled with such fatal results by Allan and Clara so many years before. On the night of Sunday 15 January, an intruder broke into her house, obviously intent on robbery, and brutally murdered the old woman by strangling her with a handkerchief round the neck. The killer tried to arrange the body as if Mrs Oliver had taken her own life, but she had put up a fight, and bruises elsewhere on her flesh told a different story. Due to the remoteness of the place itself, it took the authorities only a short time to line up a likely suspect.

The guilty man proved to be Anthony Lingard, a young fellow of twenty-one from the neighbouring hamlet of Litton. Having killed the old woman, he had stolen money and a new pair of red shoes from the house. The latter, in a remarkably stupid gesture, were presented to his pregnant girlfriend. In return, Lingard wanted her to claim the child was fathered by someone else, but his foolish action was to cost him his life. The girl refused, turned down his stolen 'gifts', and promptly betrayed him to the authorities; by the end of the month Lingard was in Derby gaol. He had tried to hide the shoes in a haystack, and later inside his house, but once more he was out of luck. Samuel Marsden, the cobbler from Stoney Middleton who had made the shoes confirmed he had sold them to Hannah Oliver, and added that they contained a piece of packing on which the prophetic words 'commit no crime' were printed. Once the shoes were discovered and prised open, the incriminating paper was found, and Lingard was doomed. Like so many before and after, he was hanged at Derby on 28 March 1815. As a grim postscript, his body was carried back by a group of soldiers to Wardlow Mires, to be exposed on the gibbet close to the scene of the murder, at a place now known as Gibbet Field.

The gibbet, a punishment where the bodies of criminals were hung in chains or inside a metal cage until they decayed and disintegrated, had been in use since the Middle Ages, and sometimes the condemned men had been placed there while still alive. The last live victim of the Derbyshire gibbet was an unnamed homicidal tramp, who in the seventeenth century murdered an old woman who refused him food by pouring hot bacon fat down her throat. For this horrible crime he suffered an equally appalling death, and was hung up alive on Gibbet Moor, near to Chatsworth House, home of the Duke of Devonshire. Evidently the man's screams disturbed the Duke so much that live gibbeting was discontinued, but clearly there were no objections to dead wrongdoers suffering the same fate. Gibbeting was intended as a particularly unpleasant deterrent to would-be criminals. Unfortunately, like the public executions

The bleak landscape of Wardlow Mires, where the victims of Derbyshire's last gibbet were left on display to passers-by. Dennis Middleton

that continued until later in the nineteenth century, it was seen by many as a form of entertainment, and large crowds flocked to see Lingard's dangling corpse as it was exhibited for the first time on April Fool's Day, a Sunday. John Longden, a Methodist lay preacher, arrived at his Tideswell church to find it empty, as everyone had gone to Wardlow to view Lingard's remains. Longden walked on to Gibbet Field himself, and there beneath the decomposing corpse of the murderer delivered a reproving sermon to his errant flock. One suspects that it made little difference.

There were some, however, that took no pleasure from the spectacle. William Newton, a poet born in the nearby village of Abney, was so disgusted by what he saw that he penned verses of his own demanding the abolition of the gibbet, and the obscene carnival atmosphere it attracted. His poem won over a substantial body of public opinion, and after a while the gibbet was demolished, what was left of Anthony Lingard was taken down and buried. He was the last Derbyshire criminal to suffer this terrible fate.

Chapter 9

The Government Opposed Must Be
1817

On the night of 9 June 1817 a group of desperate men from the village of Pentrich and the hamlets round about set out from Hunt's Farm at Wingfield Park in search of weapons and recruits to their cause. With no hope of work, and virtually starving from lack of food, all were resolved that things had to change. In order to achieve this, in the words of one of their songs, they were agreed that 'the government opposed must be'. Driven to violent rebellion, they aimed to capture Nottingham and help to overthrow the unpopular government of Lord Liverpool. Sadly, their misguided efforts would result only in the death of a harmless bystander, and their leaders would pay with their own lives on the Derby gallows.

In 1815, when the corpse of Anthony Lingard was gibbeted at Wardlow Mires, the Napoleonic Wars were coming to an end. Unfortunately, like other wars before and since, the end of conflict saw a slump in those industries geared to wartime production. Iron-working and framework knitting, the livelihood of many Pentrich men, had been hard hit by the post-war recession.

To make matters worse, everything else seemed to be going wrong, too, including the weather. Recent scientific research has shown that the eruption of the Tambora volcano in 1815 had a devastating effect worldwide, and the climate became unseasonably cold. Derbyshire experienced snow in June 1815, and bad weather ruined harvests the following year. By 1817 many working people, in Derbyshire and elsewhere, were close to starvation. Nor did the government offer any hope of salvation. Lord Liverpool had removed the *Habaeus Corpus* act which prevented imprisonment without trial, and Parliament no longer represented the people of a country greatly changed by the movement of rural workers to the cities. Dissident groups

Pentrich Village Hall, the former home of the radical Thomas Bacon at the time of the Pentrich Revolution in 1817. Dennis Middleton

had begun to appear, dedicated to the overthrow of their rulers. Hampden clubs, named after the Civil War rebel John Hampden, met in Ripley and Derby, and their doctrines spread to the outlying villages.

One of these radicals, Thomas Bacon, lived at Pentrich, and had recently returned from Yorkshire with word that a revolution was planned, involving men from Yorkshire and the Midlands, who would converge on London and remove Lord Liverpool and his friends from power. Soon the men of the village were being urged to take part in this armed uprising. Most of Bacon's recruits were not too politically minded; at a time when families were starving due to ruined harvests, food was far more important, and his promise of food and money struck a responsive chord. By 1817 links had been established with similar Nottinghamshire organisations, and a new leader was sent across the border to Pentrich. This was Jeremiah Brandreth, an out-of-work stockinger from Sutton-in-Ashfield, whose code-name was 'the Nottingham captain'. He addressed a meeting at the *White Horse* public house, and informed those present of the plan. The uprising was to take place on 9 June, when the rebels would march on to Nottingham, seizing weapons and press-ganging local recruits on the way. With Brandreth in charge, the would-be revolutionaries were hopeful of success.

Unfortunately, as with Anthony Babington three hundred years before, the government was already ahead of them. Most of the neighbouring groups had been infiltrated and destroyed by the time the Pentrich men were ready to move, and their own organisation contained a spy by the name of Oliver, who was busily reporting back to his superiors. The result was that Lord Liverpool was fully aware of what Brandreth and the others intended before they made a move. At 10 pm on 9 June the rebels left Hunt's Barn and began their march, waking the inhabitants of outlying farms and trying to gain recruits. They had scant success, and at one farm the owner – Widow Hepworth – refused to open up to them. An argument ensued between Brandreth and the defiant widow and her sons, and at its height someone – whether Brandreth himself, or another rebel, is open to question - fired a pistol through a rear window. A servant,

The Dog Inn, *formerly* The Spaniel Dog, *Pentrich*. Dennis Middleton

Robert Walters, was struck by the pistol ball as he was tying his boot-laces, and died instantly. He was to be the only casualty inflicted by the Pentrich rebels.

Rebuffed at the Hepworth Farm, Brandreth led his force on to the Butterley Iron Works, where he arrived with some 500 men. Butterley Works would have provided him with a very useful arsenal, but this time he was met by the manager Mr Goodwin, who refused to let him pass. With 500 men behind him, Brandreth could easily have captured the place, but incredibly he allowed Goodwin to browbeat him, and turned away to continue the march.

From this point on, things went from bad to worse. The march degenerated into a glorified pub-crawl, the disorganised rebels drinking at several public houses along the route and promising to pay when they returned victorious. It poured with rain, and many of the marchers, guessing their venture had no chance of success, began to slink off home. Brandreth and the greatly reduced remnant crossed into Nottinghamshire, where at Giltbrook they found a unit of cavalry waiting for them. At the first onset, the dispirited rebels broke and ran, and before long most of them were hunted down and captured. Determined to make an example of them, the government put on a 'show trial' at Derby County Hall that lasted for ten days. Jeremiah Brandreth and two of the other leaders, William Turner and Isaac Ludlam, were sentenced to be hanged, drawn and quartered, the same savage fate allotted by Elizabeth I to the Babington conspirators. Six of the luckier rebels were imprisoned, and fourteen transported to Australia. Twelve others were brought to trial, but no evidence was found against them, and they were freed. The executions of the Pentrich leaders took place at Derby on 7 November 1817. In the end, Brandreth and the other two condemned men escaped the worst of the sentence, the government relenting sufficiently to have them 'merely' hanged and beheaded. A crowd of 6,000 watched them die, among them the radical poet Percy Bysshe Shelley, who later made his sympathies known in verse.

For Brandreth, Ludlam and Turner the punishment was over, but for the other rebels and their families it had hardly begun.

THE

TRIALS

OF

JEREMIAH BRANDRETH,
WILLIAM TURNER, ISAAC LUDLAM,
GEORGE WEIGHTMAN,

AND OTHERS,

FOR

High Treason,

UNDER A SPECIAL COMMISSION AT DERBY,

ON

Thursday the 16th,
Friday the 17th,
Saturday the 18th,
Monday the 20th,
Tuesday the 21st,
Wednesday the 22d,
Thursday the 23d,
Friday the 24th, and
Saturday the 25th of October, 1817.

WITH THE ANTECEDENT PROCEEDINGS.

IN TWO VOLUMES:—VOL. I.

TAKEN IN SHORT HAND BY
WILLIAM BRODIE GURNEY,
Short Hand Writer to both Houses of Parliament.

London:

SOLD BY BUTTERWORTH AND SON, FLEET STREET, AND
FENNER, PATERNOSTER ROW.

1817.

Title page from The Trials of Jeremiah Brandreth, William Turner, Isaac Ludlam, George Weightman, and others, for High Treason, under a Special Commission at Derby, 1817. Chesterfield Local Studies Library

Their homes were demolished and the families evicted, their land awarded to more 'loyal' tenants. Years later, bitterness still smouldered between the descendants of the dispossessed and those who had taken their places in the village. Ironically, some of those transported to Australia seem to have fared better than the rest, making new lives for themselves on the far side of the world. In Derbyshire, the last of the rebels is believed to have been Charles Booth, who after four marriages and years in a thriving draper's business, died in 1896 at the ripe old age of ninety-seven! But that was to be much later. For the crushed revolutionaries, the years ahead offered only bitterness and hardship. It was not until 1832 and the Reform Bill that the government did away with the worst of its oppression, and by then they must have long regretted taking part in that ill-fated rising on 9 June 1817.

Chapter 10

The Shocking Affair at Whittington
1845

To the north-east of Chesterfield lies the district of Whittington. It consists of the main village of Old Whittington, its north-eastern neighbour New Whittington, and the southern area of Whittington Moor, once the location for the annual Chesterfield Races. Whittington has been part of Chesterfield borough since 1920, but in Victorian times existed as an independent parish. It was here, in March 1845, that a particularly shocking murder was enacted.

In the centre of Old Whittington village lived Mrs Elizabeth Green, the widow of a local farmer. Her house was within walking distance of the *Cock and Magpie Inn,* which in 1688 had served as a venue for the Duke of Devonshire and his co-conspirators in their plotting to overthrow James II in the

The Cock and Magpie, *Old Whittington, where Elizabeth Green went in vain for help on the day of the murder in 1845.* Dennis Middleton

'Glorious Revolution'. Mrs Green was still owner of her late husband's farm, but the land was worked by her son-in-law, Joseph Hawksley, who was married to her eldest daughter. The couple had seven children. Hawksley had previously lived in Hackenthorpe, a north Derbyshire village later to become part of South Yorkshire, but in April 1844 had moved to Whittington. His home was now part of Mrs Green's house, a large building which had been divided into two separate dwellings, and he worked the fifteen-acre farm as her tenant.

The situation, itself far from ideal, had been made a good deal worse by a clash of personalities. It was later to emerge that neither Hawksley nor Mrs Green had an unblemished past. The former, while living in Hackenthorpe, had been guilty of several thefts, including stealing money from the pit banks, for which offence he had been subjected to a horse-whipping. On the other side, Mrs Green had previously been convicted as a receiver of stolen goods; the thief, one of her sons, had been sentenced to transportation to Australia. For some time it had been evident that Hawksley did not get on with his mother-in-law, and several confrontations involving threats and bad language had been witnessed by others in the village. The war of words had been taken up a further notch by another of Mrs Green's sons, who had apparently caused malicious damage to a plough that Hawksley was using on the farm, for which he was later fined. About the same time both Mrs Green and her son-in-law were brought before the Magistrates, and the widow appealed for them to bind Hawksley over to keep the peace. Her application was refused, and both parties received a reprimand. On the evening of 12 March 1845 Hawksley, apparently the worse for drink, had tried to force his way into his mother-in-law's house, ostensibly to show her a paper relating to the farm's tillages, but was prevented from entering by her son, Sydney Green. It was the last time Sydney was to see his mother alive.

The following morning, Thursday 13 March, Mrs Green was seen by several neighbours prior to 10 am, one of whom reported that she was cleaning her stone doorstep. Shortly afterwards she went into the house, only to be seen running out with both hands clutching her throat. She staggered to the door of the *Cock and Magpie*, then on to another nearby house, but could find no-one to help her. Returning to her own house, she collapsed, and when her neighbours found her she lay sprawled on the stones of the yard, unable to speak as blood poured from a deep gash in her throat.

The alarm was raised and the surgeon, William Edward Boddington, was summoned. On arriving, he found Mrs Green lying on the hearth in her kitchen. With the help of his assistant and the women in the room he lifted her on to the table to examine her. She was already dead, and the cause was not hard to find. The deep wound in her throat, extending from ear to ear, had partially severed the oesophagus and jugular vein, and the carotid artery, although not cut, was laid bare. Mr Boddington noticed that an old horn-handled razor lay open on the ground by the corpse, stained with blood on the handle and blade. The surgeon questioned those present as to who could give him information, and was directed to ask Hawksley, who now entered the room.

Hawksley claimed he had been working in a nearby field when he heard a scream, and ran down to his own house, thinking the young children there might have accidentally burned themselves. He said he saw Mrs Green cross her garden in the direction of the street, but as there seemed to be nothing wrong with her he went down his own yard towards the street. At this point he realised that his mother-in-law was bleeding badly, and helped her back to the house, but that she fell on the step. Then the neighbours had arrived, and carried her inside. Boddington asked him if anyone had seen him in the field, to which Hawksley replied 'Yes, the messenger I sent you.' The surgeon responded to this by assuring him that, 'if any person saw you in the field, it is of no consequence to you.' Hawksley, though, was obviously still troubled, and prior to Boddington's departure, when only he and his assistant were present, the farmer let slip the disturbing comment that 'it is very unfortunate for me, because my being unfriendly with her, people may say I've done it.'

It was indeed unfortunate for Joseph Hawksley that, while no witness could be found to verify his presence in the field, more than one claimed to have seen him in and around Mrs Green's house just prior to her death. Hawksley's own behaviour at the time did not help matters. When Whittington's parish constable John Naylor made for the scene of the crime on Thursday morning, he was met by Hawksley. Naylor immediately demanded if he (Hawksley) had done the killing, and the latter protested his innocence, but behaved in an evasive manner. When Naylor told him to return with him to the house, Hawksley agreed, but then hung back and did not follow.

Hawksley had clearly emerged as the prime suspect, and on Friday 14 March he was arrested by Naylor, the Whittington constable, and C Cotterill, one of the constables from the Chesterfield Borough police force formed in the early 1830s. Hawksley was apprehended at the *Rising Sun Inn*, on the Moor, in Sheffield, and it was discovered that he had gone to Sheffield to inquire about the late Mrs Green's will, which stated that her property was to be divided equally between her children, of whom Hawksley's wife was the eldest. This latest development only served to render his behaviour even more open to question, and on Wednesday 19 March he appeared before the Chesterfield Magistrates Edward Gilling Maynard and John Meynell, on suspicion of murdering his mother-in-law six days before. The hearing was not open to the public, and Mr Maynard was at pains to point out that on this occasion they were here not to try Hawksley, but 'merely to examine whether the case ought to be sent for trial.' To this end, a number of witnesses were called.

Julia Baxby, a neighbour, had delivered milk to Mrs Green before 9 am and found her in good health, eating her breakfast. Mrs Green had given her money to fetch half a stone of flour, and asked the loan of two household items. An hour later, James Shepley had come into Miss Baxby's house and told her something was wrong with Mrs Green, 'for there's as much blood on the causeway as would fill a bowl.' This last remark so frightened Miss Baxby that she dared not go outside, and did not witness the widow's death.

Mr Boddington, the surgeon, then gave evidence, describing the razor he had seen, and the nature of the wound. 'The wound was in the throat: it was about four inches in length, and had evidently been produced by a sharp cutting instrument which had opened the internal jugular vein on the left side, and also some small branches of the external carotid artery. It had also opened the oesophagus, or the tube leading from the stomach to the windpipe. I had no doubt that the wound was the cause of death.' Pressed as to whether the injury was by another hand, or self-inflicted, he replied that the deceased could have inflicted such a wound on herself. Although not certain, Mr Boddington felt that the blow had been struck from left to right, and was consistent with the use of the razor found in the kitchen. He also reported his conversation with Hawksley, and the comments that had been made to him.

A young boy, Richard Montgomery, who had been playing near the house that fateful morning, remembered seeing Hawksley with Mrs Green in the Town street, below the elder trees, between 9 am and 10 am. Mrs Green had blood on her arms, and fell down twenty yards from her step. She then sat up, and pushed Hawksley off the causeway. Richard had often seen them quarrelling before. So had most of the other witnesses. Hannah Moody, the boy's grandmother, had been one of those who ran to help the dying woman. Her daughter, Hannah Montgomery, and Hawksley himself had carried the widow into the house and laid her on the hearth. Mrs Moody said that Mrs Green had turned to her and tried to tell her something, but Mrs Moody could not understand her. Mrs Etty Cook, who was also present, claimed that she had heard the words, uttered in a low voice 'It's him! It's him!' while Hawksley was there. Mrs Moody had seen the razor, which stayed untouched until Naylor, the parish constable, took charge of it. She also claimed that when Hawksley had tried to lift the victim's head, Mrs Green had pushed his hand away, but did nothing to stop the women touching her. Both she and her daughter noted blood on the floor, and bloody finger-prints on the bolts and handle of the back door, and a bit of ribbon that lay some distance from the body. None of those questioned felt that Mrs Green showed any indication of wanting to take her own life.

William Linley, a carpenter in the village, recalled a visit to the home of the deceased one Saturday afternoon about six weeks ago. Invited to sit down and smoke his pipe, he then heard a violent crash on the door, and Hawksley was heard to shout 'Turn that old thief out, you old bitch and whore!' He and Mrs Green went outside, to find Hawksley looking at them over the wall and threatening to kill them both. His recollection of an earlier incident in November 1844 seemed grimly prophetic. Linley was carrying some coals to the widow's house, and Hawksley tried to stop him. As they squabbled, Hawksley called out to Mrs Green 'Why don't you get a black gown and go into mourning? Your time is not long, and before I go I shall follow you to the grave.' He had also threatened Linley's life on another occasion. Sarah Wall recounted a not dissimilar story. She had lived with Mrs Green for about seven months, and only recently left. During that time she had seen many quarrels, and once when she and the widow were outside shaking carpets Hawksley had told Mrs Green 'You damned old bitch, you'll not be surprised if you're smothered in the house before morning. I shall see you taken to the church-yard before I leave yet.' On another occasion, the two of them had seen Hawksley press his face up to the window as they sat in the kitchen, and soon afterwards Mrs Wall said she heard what sounded like a shot, but when she went to investigate, he had disappeared. She also claimed that Hawksley had been given notice to quit by Mrs Green, and that she had seen the notice herself.

Charles Shepherd, a cordwainer (shoemaker) who lived nearby, stated that about 9 am on the morning of 13 March he was wheeling ashes out of his father's garden, when he heard Hawksley call his name. Turning round, he saw Hawksley standing by the gate in his field. When Shepherd went to meet him he heard a scream from Mrs Green's house, a cry he thought to have been made by her young grandson, John Green. Shepherd got over the wall into the field, and followed Hawksley in the direction of the sound. He saw Mrs Green fall down near the steps, but had not seen Hawksley near her before then, although he knew they had quarrelled at other times. The magistrates felt they had sufficient cause to detain Hawksley, and he was remanded until Monday 24 March, bail having been refused. The adjourned examination was resumed on that

Revolution House, OldWhittington. This building, where the Duke of Devonshire and others plotted to overthrow James II in 1688, would have been only yards from the murder scene a century and a half later. Dennis Middleton

date, and this time the public were admitted, the witnesses once more giving their evidence. Though much of it was circumstantial, none of it helped Hawksley's case. Several women were able to corroborate that Mrs Green had pushed him away, and that she had tried to say something to them. And there was worse to come.

Frederick Stainton Hodges, Mr Boddington's assistant, testified that he had noticed flecks of blood on the right wristband of Hawksley's shirt while they were in the house, and had later mentioned this to the surgeon on the way back to Chesterfield. Samuel Hollingworth, keeper of the lock-up where Hawksley had been confined, testified that the previous evening the prisoner had told him that the real killer was a local man, Mark Siddall; the following morning, questioned by Hollingworth, he denied ever having made such a claim. Samuel Siddall, joiner and wheelwright, stated that around 9.30 am on the morning in question he was working on a waggon in Mr Jenkinson's field when he heard a scream. Looking round, he saw a man in light-coloured clothes run up from Mrs Green's and Hawksley's house to a gate in the field, and heard him call out 'Charley!' A second man he assumed to be Shepherd got over the wall. He also saw a woman and child coming up Town street towards Mrs Green's gate, and while on the way they were overtaken by the first man he had seen. Following a short time later, Siddall saw Hawksley come out of the house. Interest also focused on the razor found in the house. It had been claimed that Mrs Green used it to cut her corns, but this was denied by Elizabeth Newton, who stated that the weapon found was definitely not the razor normally used by the deceased. Throughout the proceedings Hawksley kept trying to interrupt the witnesses, accusing them of lying and proclaiming his innocence. When permitted to speak at the close, he claimed that 'he never touched her', and that he would explain everything to the magistrates if they would visit him the following morning. This was agreed, and he was committed to face trial for wilful murder at the next Assizes.

Meanwhile, an inquest was held at the *Cock and Magpie*, J Hutchinson being the coroner. Julia Baxby, Samuel Siddall, Charles Shepherd, Etty Cook, Richard Montgomery and his mother Hannah once more gave evidence. The last-named recalled the pitiful sight of young John Green sitting by his dying grandmother, begging her to speak to him. The inquest was adjourned, and resumed on Tuesday 25 March, when more witnesses were called. George Widdowson, a shoemaker, had seen Mrs Green come out of her house with the wound in her throat, a sight which had caused his wife to faint. John Green was with his grandmother, and Widdowson claimed that the boy stood on the threshold and said 'my uncle did it' before following Mrs Green. The coroner immediately pointed out that this did not constitute evidence.

All the same, things looked bad for the accused. Sydney Green, the son of the dead woman, informed Mr Hutchinson that he and Constable Naylor had searched Hawksley's house and found a razor there, but it was clear that it had not been used for some time. The horn-handled razor at the scene of the crime was one Green had often seen in Hawksley's house, both here in Whittington and previously at his home in Hackenthorpe. Mr Boddington, the surgeon, was also called, and gave his opinion that it would have been possible for Mrs Green, resting her head on her chest, to communicate in a whisper in spite of her wound, a statement that appeared to back up the claims of Hannah Moody and Etty Cook. The boy, John Green, also gave evidence which was 'given with striking clearness and consistency.' Summing up, Mr Hutchinson reviewed the evidence, and informed the jury that they must decide on a verdict of suicide or wilful murder. The jurors withdrew, then returned with a verdict of wilful murder against Joseph Hawksley.

Hawksley, however, did not live to stand trial. Following the examination on Monday 24 March he was once more confined in the House of Correction at Chesterfield. The keeper, Samuel Hollingworth, had each evening been careful to remove his neckerchief and garters to prevent possible suicide, but on Monday evening this must have escaped his notice. At 6 pm he spoke to Hawksley, who appeared to behave normally. Returning at 6.45 pm, Hollingworth opened the cell door to find Hawksley suspended from the band on the hinge by his neckerchief. Horrified, the lock-up keeper cut him down, but it was already too late. Joseph Hawksley had been strangled to death by the neckerchief, which had cut so tightly into his neck that the fibres were embedded in the flesh. A subsequent inspection of the cell revealed messages scratched into the walls accusing Siddall and protesting his own innocence, together with the final plaintive comment 'I cannot live in this place no longer.'

When the jury visited the House of Correction to view the body, it showed no signs of violent death, and 'the countenance was tolerably placid.' A prayer-book was found in the cell, lying open and with some leaves removed, topped by a pair of spectacles. The passage visible to the jury was from Psalm 73, and ran:

> *Until I went into the sanctuary of God, thus understood I the end of these men; Namely, how thou dost set them in slippery places, and castedst them down, and destroyedst them. Oh, how suddenly do they consume, perish, and come to a fearful end.*

At the inquest on Hawksley, on Wednesday 26 March at the *Commercial Hotel* in Chesterfield, the Coroner pointed out to the jurors that if they decided that Hawksley had killed himself while insane, he would not only be deprived of Christian burial but he and his wife would forfeit all their property. With this in mind, he directed them to bring a verdict that there was no evidence as to the state of Hawksley's mind at the time of his death. The verdict was duly returned, and this welcome touch of humanity brought the shocking affair at Whittington to a close.

Chapter 11

The Cesspit Horror
1845

On the chill winter evening of Sunday 7 December 1845, George Collis went missing. A young man of twenty-six, he had originally worked as a servant to the Barnes family, land and coal-owners, at Ashgate House on the western side of town, but had since gone into partnership with a local butcher, John Platts. Platts leased premises from a Mr Parker in the area of central Chesterfield known as the Shambles. This cluster of shops and public houses immediately east of the Market Place and close to the warren of yards leading off Low Pavement had been a feature of the town from medieval times. It took its name from its long service as a venue for butchering livestock, and its dark, cramped alleys and buildings made it an unhealthy and dangerous place. By early Victorian times it was the regular scene of drunken violence and the sight of prostitutes plying their trade, and the inns and shops attracted a rough-and-ready clientele. Some of the owners of premises, too, were not immune to illegal activities.

Collis had invested his savings in the business, while Platts provided the butchering expertise, but by the night of 7 December it was plain that this arrangement was not working. Apparently Platts owed Collis money, and the latter had set up a meeting with him and some other acquaintances that night, and prior to keeping his appointment he was seen alive by at least three people. His mother, Mrs Mary Mawles, recalled seeing him off from their house that afternoon, and clearly remembered the clothes he was wearing. George was dressed in a black cloth surtout (overcoat), canary-yellow waistcoat, and a black silk handkerchief bearing his initials. On his legs he wore two garters, a white knitted one and another with a red binding, and he carried a buff canvas purse. Later, at about 6.20 pm, George called on his sweetheart, a young woman called Ellen Beresford.

He stayed only for five minutes or so, telling her that he intended to collect the money from Platts, and then to go on to Manchester, presumably to establish himself in a fresh line of business. Ellen, who was already expecting his child, had herself previously been in service at Ashgate, where she and her lover had first met, and the garters he wore were a present from her. Before leaving, he consulted his watch and checked the time at 6.25 pm. From what he told her, Ellen felt that George Collis already feared for his life. Another who saw Collis was Catherine Franks, landlady of the *Old Angel Inn*, who remembered him entering the hostelry together with Platts in the course of the evening. Some time later, Platts came back alone, and it was noted that he had a badly cut hand.

John Heathcoate, a joiner from Lordsmill Street, was heading towards the Shambles around 6.30 pm when he saw Collis leave Ellen's house, and himself make his way to the Shambles via Packers Row. Continuing on his way, Heathcoate heard a noise and looking round saw Collis and Platts standing in the shop of Henry Morley, another butcher. Platts, a stout young man standing only 4 feet 11 inches high, was holding a hammer which he struck against a bench. Heathcoate walked on, and as he did so he seemed to hear the sounds of a scuffle, followed by a noise 'as if something had fallen over a bucket and knocked it over'. The door of the shop was slammed shut and fastened. The

The Shambles, Chesterfield, with the Royal Oak *in the foreground. This dark, dangerous area of town, with its maze of yards and alleys, was where James Collis met his end in 1845.* Dennis Middleton

Low Pavement, showing the distinctive half-timbered Peacock Inn, *which John Heathcote had just left when he saw three men carrying a mysterious bundle from the Shambles into Falcon Yard.* Dennis Middleton

following evening, Heathcote was on his way from his club at the *Peacock Inn* on Low Pavement intending to meet his brother Godfrey. He caught sight of three men coming out of a butcher's shop in the Shambles and crossing Low Pavement for Bunting's Yard (today's Falcon Yard) carrying a bundle roughly five feet long, which to Heathcote looked like 'a sheep pack'. They disappeared into the yard, and some time later two of them came out minus the bundle. Heathcote then met his brother and they continued on their way, dismissing the incident from their minds. There were others who would later report unusual events they had witnessed on the night of 7 December.

Samuel Slack, of Brampton, en route to his sister's public house, the *Bull's Head*, in the Shambles, saw two men pushing a third, who appeared to be heavily drunk or dazed and unsteady on his feet, into John Platts' shop. The man fell down inside the shop, and the other two went in and locked the door behind them.

Thomas Harvey, on his way to visit relatives on the occasion of a friend's wedding in the Shambles, passed Platts' premises, and as he did so heard what sounded like blows and a moaning noise. When he arrived at his in-laws, the Bellamys, he remarked on what he had heard, and all three went back to the shop, and Mrs Bellamy called out asking Platts who was in there with him. The voice of Platts replied that no-one else was there. Bellamy, thinking Platts had his girlfriend Hannah inside, threatened to break down the door, but was dissuaded. Platts claimed he had drunk some rum and felt sick, but would soon be better. Bellamy thought he heard a noise as if Platts was dragging something heavy across the floor. James Kirk, a butcher, was also with the Bellamys and Harvey, and backed up their story. Kirk had threatened to smash the door down, thinking Hannah to be inside, but Platts reassured him, and in fact they found out that Hannah was in church at the time. Later on that night Platts came to the Bellamy's house. They noticed his face was very flushed, and he had a cut on his hand, which was washed and bound up. They joked about his relationship with Hannah, and he mentioned that Collis had gone to Manchester while owing him money. He also said he had put in a raffle at Mansfield.

John Holbrook, owner of an eating house in the Shambles, remembered meeting Collis on that night between 6 pm and 7 pm, when the latter paid him 8d. They agreed to meet at a house in Brampton at 9 pm, but Collis never turned up. Holbrook waited until midnight, and on returning to the Shambles saw a light in Platts' shop and heard something moving. Cloths were fastened over the doors, so it was impossible to see inside. He recalled that on Monday the shop stayed shut all day, as he had passed it several times.

Once Collis's absence was noted, suspicion seems to have fallen immediately on John Platts. The blacksmith Edward Parsons remembered the undersized butcher coming into his shop on Monday 8 December to obtain some meat-hooks, and Parsons told him he was suspected of murder by Thomas Harvey. Platts laughed this off, explaining away the suspicious noise by claiming he had fallen on a lantern and cut himself while trying to open a shutter. Whatever people thought, no body could be produced, and it seemed reasonable to assume that Collis had gone to Manchester as he had intended. Slowly the excitement died down, and George Collis's disappearance was forgotten.

Several months later, on 28 August 1846, Valentine Wall and Richard Ashley were busy cleaning out the cesspit in Bunting's Yard. Two privies emptied into it, and it was also used as a handy place for other 'illegal dumping' by the inhabitants of the Shambles. The stench on the hot August day can only be imagined, but worse was to come. Wall's shovel hit against

Falcon Yard, where nightsoil workers discovered the corpse of George Collis in a cesspit. Dennis Middleton

something hard, and he dug up what at first he thought was a sheep's carcass. On closer inspection, it proved to be the bones and the remnants of clothing of what had once been a man. He and Ashley lifted it, at which 'three parts fell away'. Ashley stated that 'they got a coat, trowsers, a hat, two thigh bones and two leg bones fastened together at the end. The flesh came off the bones into his hand, and fell into the soil.' The ghastly find was loaded on to a cart, which set it down in a field owned by Mr Bunting. The carter Thomas Green remembered seeing trousers, neckerchief and garters round the leg bones, one white and the other red.

The remains were examined by the surgeon, Mr Walker, prior to being given to the constable of Hasland. Mr Walker verified that they were the bones of a man between twenty-three and thirty. He noted a five-inch fracture of the forehead, another near the left eyebrow, and a third across the base of the skull, all consistent with blows from a sharp cutting instrument. The blows would have been fatal, although the victim might have taken some time to die. Apart from a few neck bones and three ribs, the skeleton was complete. The fragments of clothing were enough to confirm that the body was that of George Collis, a fact established at the coroner's inquest on 3 September, when several of the witnesses already mentioned gave evidence.

Platts had always been under suspicion. Some weeks before, a police officer had searched his premises in the hope of finding items stolen from his previous employer, Mr Statham, and found a yellow purse and a pawn ticket for a watch, but these had vanished when the constable returned. The watch had been redeemed by Platts' mother from Wilcockson the pawn-broker, and Platts, who was now taken into custody, informed the keeper of the lock-up where it might be found. The watch was recovered from Platts' house, under a stone bench in the pantry, hidden under brick-ends and broken pots. Platts denied the murder, and claimed he bought the watch from 'Lanky Bill'.

He was brought to trial at Derby Crown Court on Friday 19 March 1847, where he was charged with the wilful murder of George Collis. Evidence was heard from all key witnesses, including William Beaumont, the 'Lanky Bill' from whom Platts claimed to have bought the watch. Beaumont, officially a labourer but engaged in the more lucrative unofficial business of brothel-keeping, shared a house with two known prostitutes. A member of Chesterfield's underworld, he had previously been lodged in Derby gaol three or four times. He had not, however, sold the watch to Platts. This was duly confirmed by the watchmaker John Thompson of Chesterfield, who identified the item as one he had sold 'to a person named Collis' on 29 December 1839. Ellen Beresford identified the same watch, together with the garters and handkerchief, as those of her former lover. Circumstantial evidence, but it all pointed in Platts' direction. The jury found him guilty of murder, and he was sentenced to be hanged.

To the end, Platts denied the actual killing of Collis, although he admitted to being a member in the conspiracy to murder him. His confession implicated the butcher Henry Morley and Anthony Launt as his fellows in the plan. In this account, which does not tie in with the evidence of the witnesses, he claimed that 'Morley and I laid the plan before dinner, after the people were gone into church. He said he had been with (Launt) and they had laid a plan to make away with Collis.' The motive for the crime was that Collis owed money to Morley for slaughtered animals, and Platts owed money to Collis. Platts said that it was agreed that Morley should strike the first blow, being the strongest, and that Platts and Launt should help finish off their victim by strangling him. Bearing in mind how small Platts himself was, this is perhaps not too hard to believe. He claimed that Morley killed Collis in a stable, using a spade, and that he (Platts) witnessed the third blow, after which Morley strangled the luckless young man with a butcher's bleeding-cord. As for the noises at his own premises, he repeated his story of falling on the lantern and cutting himself. He stayed in on the Monday, and on Tuesday morning he and Morley put the corpse into a wheel-barrow, covered it with straw, and wheeled it into Bunting's Yard, where it was tipped into the cess-pit. The bundle seen by the Heathcoates the previous night was, according to him, totally unconnected with the crime.

Whatever the truth or otherwise of Platts' confession, there seems little doubt that Morley was involved in the murder. Unfortunately, he had already died in delirium (either of typhus or delirium tremens) three days after the inquest. Anthony Launt, another suspect, was later brought to trial but acquitted for lack of evidence. John Platts made his journey to the scaffold on 1 April 1847 outside Derby gaol, attended by the usual crowd of morbidly curious onlookers. According to the contemporary report 'He struggled hard when the drop fell - his arms and left hand moved to and fro, as far as his irons would allow, for nearly two minutes.'

At the time of his death, John Platts was twenty-two years old.

More than sixty years later, in 1911, the *Derbyshire Times* recorded the reminiscences of eighty-year-old Mr William Shipley, who had been a boy of fourteen when the crime was committed. Mr Shipley obviously had a talent as a raconteur, and introduced several fresh suggestions of his own. He claimed that Ellen Beresford had retained one of the tell-tale garters, that Collis had intended to go to America, and that Mr Statham, Platts' previous employer, was also implicated in the plot and came to a bad end. While none of these stories accords with the facts in the contemporary accounts, his comment that sheepstealing was common at the time, and that several of the butchers in the Shambles were involved in 'fencing' stolen stock sounds far more convincing. Given the background of the case, it seems more than likely that Morley and Platts, and perhaps George Collis too, were participants in shady dealing of this kind. Who knows, it may even explain the five-foot 'sheep pack' that John Heathcoate saw carried into Bunting's Yard that winter's night in 1845?

The Yards, Low Pavement, nowadays a tourist attraction, but in the nineteenth century a place to be avoided after dark. Dennis Middleton

Chapter 12

Death by the Highway
1857

By the mid-Victorian period the days of the highwayman and the footpad had all but gone. Following the establishment of the Metropolitan Police in London, the growth of borough and county forces and improved methods of detection, together with a general improvement in living standards, resulted in their decline. The largely ineffective 'Bloody Code' was gradually repealed, and the number of capital sentences greatly reduced in favour of terms of imprisonment. All the same, robbery and death by the highway had not disappeared altogether. One of the nightmare figures of the well-to-do Victorian was the 'garotter', who had become a familiar criminal threat by the 1850s. Possibly taking their inspiration from the murderous Thugs of India with their strangling cords – 1857 was also the year of the Indian Mutiny – these robbers usually operated in pairs, one attacking the victim from behind and tightening a noose or handkerchief round his neck to render him unconscious while the accomplice went through his pockets for valuables. Occasionally, whether deliberately or due to excessive enthusiasm, the victim died as a result.

On the night of Saturday 10 January 1857, between 10 pm and 11 pm, Mr Samuel Jenkinson was returning from Chesterfield to his home at Whittington. Mr Jenkinson was a local farmer and a man of substance; the wheelwright Samuel Siddall had been working on his waggon in one of his fields when he saw Joseph Hawksley near the house of Mrs Green in the 1845 murder case. Now, thirteen years later, Mr Jenkinson had come to within a few yards of his own entrance gates, when two men lunged out of the darkness and attacked him. The farmer was seized from behind and some kind of noose drawn tight around his neck, choking him, while the second man started rifling his pockets. Startled by the unexpected onslaught,

Church Street North, Old Whittington. Part of the historic rural village, where Samuel Jenkinson was the victim of a 'garotte' attack. Dennis Middleton

Mr Jenkinson had just enough time to cry out before the noose was tightened. His daughter, who had gone to bed, heard the noise and opened the window, and as the newspaper report has it 'inquired what was the matter'. Catching sight of the scuffle in the dark outside, but still not realising her father was the victim, Miss Jenkinson called out to a servant for assistance. At this point the garotters let go of the farmer and made a run for it, fleeing through the gateway of an adjoining field. The servant and Mr Jenkinson, who had now recovered himself, pursued them, but the thieves made good their escape. Checking his pockets, the farmer found that 'some silver' had been stolen, but it could have been a good deal worse. Had he not managed to cry out, and had he been waylaid further from his home, Mr Jenkinson could very easily have ended up another murder victim. Not too surprisingly, he was unable to give a description of his assailants, and the thieves were never brought to justice.

Towards the end of that same year, on Friday 13 November, a highway robber struck again. This time his method was not the noose, but the bullet, and his victim was not to be so lucky.

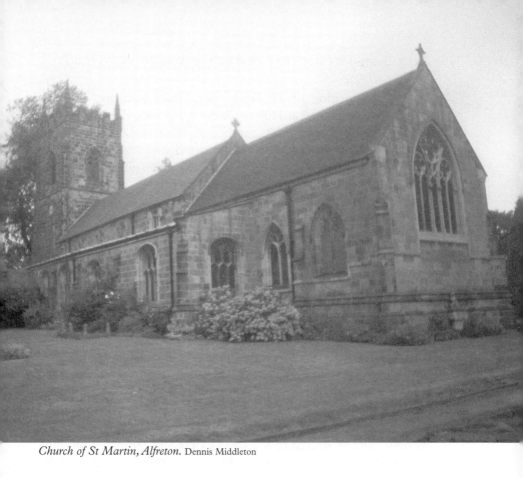

Church of St Martin, Alfreton. Dennis Middleton

Alfreton town centre. It was here that farmer James Simpson came to market for the last time on Friday, 13 November 1857. Dennis Middleton

On the morning of 13 November James Simpson left his twenty-five acre farm at Hilltop, Ashover, to walk the eight miles to Alfreton for the Friday market. A Wesleyan Reform local preacher, the thirty-six-year-old Simpson was respected in the neighbourhood as a man of industrious and sober habits. He carried a basket containing about twelve pounds of butter, and a purse with 2s 6d of silver. He was wearing an old-fashioned silver watch. Simpson intended to sell his produce at the market and to obtain some groceries, and also to conclude the sale of two fat pigs. He reached Alfreton market without incident, and witnesses later recalled meeting him there during the day.

At about 3 pm he began his return journey to Ashover, his basket now holding groceries, and with more money in his purse. On his way back, he was accompanied by Joseph Boar, a farm servant to John Gladwin of Overton Hall. The pair walked together through Shirland and Higham and as far as Ogston Hall before they parted, Boar taking the road to Woolley while Simpson continued on for Ashover Hill. Boar was later to remember that he noted the time at 3.40 pm by Ogston clock before they separated. Though Simpson was not far from home by now, the last stretch of road was lonely and remote, with only two small farms in the vicinity. At about 5 pm, less than a mile from his farm, and approaching the junction of three roads adjoined by Fabric wood at Ashover Hill Top, his journey came to a violent end. The blast of a gunshot sounded, and he fell to the ground.

For him, Friday 13 November had proved the most unlucky of days.

That same afternoon Mr Joseph Fletcher found himself walking the self-same road. Mr Fletcher was the proprietor of the nearby Alton Colliery, from which he was returning to his own home at Ashover Hill. Leaving the colliery at about 5 15 pm he made the mile-long journey to the junction of the three roads. Just before reaching the junction, Fletcher caught sight of something lying in a cart-rut in the road a dozen paces in front of him. He was about to go by, when he heard a groan, and stepped over the road for a closer look. Realising this was a man lying in the cart-rut, Fletcher at first thought he was drunk or had been thrown from his horse, but on discovering that blood was pouring from

Ashover Hilltop. The meeting place of three roads, where James Simpson was shot down from ambush on his way home from Alfreton. Dennis Middleton

Ashover Hilltop, looking to Fabric Wood. Dennis Middleton

the other's head, he called out for help.

Fortunately he was close to his own house by now, and his son Hiram and another man called Cresswell came running up within the next few minutes. Fletcher tried to speak to the injured man, but got no answer but further groans of pain. He lifted the sufferer by his shoulder, and raised his head against the bank, and sent Hiram and Cresswell to the nearby Bassett farm for help, and to call the Ashover surgeon, Mr Peter Skidmore, urging them to bring a light. After they had gone, Fletcher was joined by farm servant Joseph Marriott, and then by Mr Bassett and his nephew William, who had brought a lantern with them. By its light they saw that the injured man was James Simpson, and that he had been shot in the head. Mr Skidmore, the surgeon, arrived around 5.30 and examined Simpson as he lay in the road. He found a gunshot wound to the left temple, from which the farmer was still bleeding heavily, and there was a great deal of blood on the road. Marriott was sent to find a door to use as a makeshift stretcher, and returned with it about 6 pm. Simpson was carried back to his own house, and lingered in pain a further two hours before finally succumbing to his wound at 8.30 pm. Up to the time he died, he had not been able to speak, or give any indication who had attacked him.

By now it had been ascertained that Simpson had been robbed of 'a brown leather porte monnaie, lined with crimson or scarlet leather, about 11s or 12s in silver, and an old fashioned silver verge watch, the maker being "Plumson, London, No 8000", which was attached to a steel drop chain'. The basket, with various grocery items bought at the market, was left untouched.

Word was sent to Sergeant Gorman of the Derbyshire Constabulary, who was based at Ashover. The Derbyshire Constabulary was a new organisation, formed only the previous year in 1856, and the killing of James Simpson was to be their first high-profile murder case. The force had recruited many officers from the Royal Irish Constabulary, and Gorman, an Irish Roman Catholic, was one of several of these, including Chief Constable James Fox. He went to the murder scene and noted the heavy bloodstains on the road. He and the parish constable, Francis, attended Simpson's house, and received

Ashover Church. Dennis Middleton

confirmation that the farmer was dying. Gorman commandeered a horse and rode to Alfreton where he informed Superintendent Duncan, and details of the stolen watch were obtained from a watchmaker. Having sent a despatch to the Chief Constable, Gorman returned with Duncan to the scene of the crime, setting off on horseback at 11.30 pm, and arriving about 1 am. Duncan took a lantern and he and his sergeant searched the area. As well as the bloodstains, they found footmarks in the ground directly opposite the spot where Simpson had fallen, and signs that a gorse bush at the side of the road had been flattened by someone lying in wait. They also discovered two pieces of the kind of wadding used for the firing of small shot, close to where the victim had been lying.

A post-mortem examination of the body was made on 14

November by Mr Skidmore and fellow-surgeon Mr Marshall of Matlock. This revealed that two wounds had been inflicted, one made by a bullet and a more severe one by a slug of large swan shot. Both had entered the left side of the head between the temple and the left ear, penetrating the skull to the middle lobe of the brain. From their upward slant, and the position of the external wounds, Skidmore calculated that the shots must have been fired from Simpson's left. The damage to the skull and the extensive powder burns indicated that the gun or pistol used was fired from close range, no more than three feet away from the victim's head. Marshall was in agreement with his colleague's opinions. An inquest was held on Saturday 21 November, when Simpson's widow Hannah formally identified her husband's body and gave details of his departure for Alfreton and the items he took with him. The inquest was then adjourned until the following Tuesday to enable the police to continue their enquiries. A bill was posted on 16 November, offering £100 reward for information in apprehending the suspect, of whom a description was circulated.

The possibility that James Simpson may not have been the intended victim began to surface at the adjourned inquiry at the *White Lion Inn*, Ashover, on Tuesday 24 November, when further evidence was heard. Joseph Fletcher, who had found the dying man in the road, made the significant admission that he paid the men at Alton Colliery on Saturday afternoons, and that he normally collected the money from the bank in Chesterfield on Fridays or Saturdays, carrying it back with him to his home. Although he claimed to use a different route when taking the money home, he regularly walked the Hilltop road from the colliery on Saturday afternoon, usually getting home between 4 pm and 5 pm, the time at which the killer was lying in wait. As Mr Fletcher employed up to fifty men, the amount he might have carried – or was thought to have carried – would have been substantial, well worth a robbery attempt.

This possibility of mistaken identity was strengthened by other witnesses. On the day of the murder, about 2 pm, William Barker had been approached by a stranger as he worked in the brickyard of Alton Colliery. Having borrowed and returned a knife, the man asked if Mr Fletcher was about, and being told he was not, went off along the road leading by Fabric Wood, near the murder scene. The man was dark-skinned, 5′ 8″ or 5′ 9″ tall, with no whiskers and short-cropped hair, 'as if he was just come out of gaol'. He wore a dark blue pilot jacket with patched and ragged sleeves, cotton cord trousers, and a black cloth cap with a 'poke' in it. He appeared to be carrying something under his coat. Barker estimated his age around thirty. Both Barker and his brother-in-law, working with him, were struck by the smooth, clean, soft hands he had, 'like lady's hands', not the hands of a working man.

Barker's story was backed up by Paul Brailsford, a boy of eleven, who had been playing with two other boys and four girls at 4.40 pm that day near Ashover Hilltop, when a dark-skinned man wearing dark clothes and a 'billycock' hat came by them on the road to Simpson's house, carrying a 'barrel' (as in gunbarrel) under his clothes. The man said nothing, continuing past them out of sight.

The village of Ashover, showing the Crispin Inn. Dennis Middleton

Acting on the description from these accounts, and on further information received, Sergeant Gorman and his colleague Sergeant Hudson made an arrest. At 8 pm on Monday 23 November, the night before the resumed inquest, they apprehended the besom-maker Richard Hodgkinson at Starkholmes, near Matlock. A native of Walsall, Hodgkinson clearly fitted the description, and had been identified by a Mrs Ann Bearder as having been close to the scene of the murder on the day in question. Hodgkinson was taken into custody, and during the second inquest the boy, Paul Brailsford, was taken into a room to identify him from a group of similar men. Unfortunately for the police, Brailsford could not give a positive identification. No murder weapon was found, and in the absence of finger-printing and DNA techniques, the evidence was not enough to hold Hodgkinson on a charge of murder. He was eventually released, and the inquest jury were obliged to return an open verdict of 'wilful murder against some person or persons unknown.' To this day, the case remains unsolved. It must have been a severe disappointment for Sergeant Gorman, who had worked so hard to find the killer, but his zeal did not go unrewarded, and we shall meet him again later on. From the facts available, it would appear that the killing was a tragic case of mistaken identity, and that the murderer got the wrong man. As it happened, Mr Fletcher had not gone to the bank that week, and had he been waylaid the assassin would have killed for nothing. It is surely a supreme irony that Fletcher, the intended victim, should have been the man to find the unfortunate Simpson, shot in mistake for him as he made that fateful journey home on Friday the 13th.

Chapter 13

Killed for a Few Potatoes
1868

Murders, by their nature, are not always neatly planned. For every case of professional preparation and clinical execution, one can find numerous examples of killings committed in a sudden burst of rage or fear, where a messy, undignified scuffle had terrible consequences. Such a case was the killing of George Kelk by the young George Hughes on the night of Saturday 26 September 1868.

An attractive Georgian residence standing in its own grounds off Hasland Road, Bank Close has been the home of several leading citizens who chose to move out from Chesterfield into the leafy suburbs of the then independent parish of Hasland south of the town. Unfortunately, this pleasant-looking building houses other, darker secrets in its past, and the first of these occurred on Saturday, 26 September. At this time Bank Close was the home of Chesterfield's former mayor, Alderman William Drabble, and on the night in question he was playing host to his friends Dr and Mrs Joseph Bright of Nether Hall, Hathersage, who were staying at the house as visitors with their coachman, George Kelk.

Some time around 9.30 pm Drabble's manservant, John Holmes, was called by two female servants who had heard a noise outside. Holmes opened a door which led into the kitchen garden at the side of the house, and peered out into the dark. He couldn't see anything, but clearly heard the sound of three blows, as though someone was hitting the lattice with a stick. Closing the door carefully, he went back to the dining-room and told Mr Drabble and Mrs Drabble and their guests what was happening. Drabble went to the side door, while Bright and Holmes took up sticks and went out through the front door. As they did so Holmes saw a man making for the Hasland Road by the long carriage drive. When he was a couple of yards from the

The entrance to Bank Close House. Dennis Middleton

door, Holmes and Bright closed in on him and held him by both his arms.

The young man, who though not drunk appeared to have been drinking, claimed to have lost his way. He gave them the false name of 'Simon Burns', and told them he came from Grassmoor, a nearby village in Hasland parish. His captors found that his pockets were full of potatoes, which he claimed he had bought, but which were quite evidently just dug up from the kitchen garden near the house. Dr Bright was worried by what he described as the man's 'silly' behaviour, and obviously thought the thief had some kind of mental problem. He decided that 'Burns' should be locked up for the night for his own protection, and they turned back for the house. A short distance from it, they met George Kelk, the coachman, who was coming up to the house from the main road, carrying a parcel. Dr Bright told him they were holding a man who 'could not give a proper account of himself', and instructed Kelk and Holmes to take him to the police. Bright then returned to the house, taking the parcel, and Kelk and Holmes accompanied their captive down the drive towards the gates. It was now about 9.45 pm.

Holmes saw three men and three women walking past the gates. These were the colliers Benjamin Bamford, George Burnam and William Nuttall and their wives. They were returning home from a visit to the public house, and most, if not all of them, were in an inebriated state. Recognising Bamford, Holmes called out to him and asked if he could hold the prisoner and perhaps identify him. Bamford scrambled over the four foot wall to join them. He grabbed the man's chin to lift his head, then tugged at his neck with the neckerchief 'Burns' wore. The latter began to cry, and Kelk told Bamford not to hurt him. One of the women in the party suggested that the man they held was 'Gorley', and there was some agreement from the others, though not by everyone. It then began to rain hard, and the lightly-clad Holmes thought he had better go back and get a topcoat and umbrella. Asking the group to stay with Kelk and keep an eye on 'Burns', he hurried back to the house. It was an error that would have fatal results for Kelk.

By now the group of men and women had moved away from 'Burns' and stood outside the gates on the causeway, while Kelk

The long drive leading to Bank Close House, down which Kelk came walking on his final journey. Dennis Middleton

stayed close to the prisoner. All at once the man broke away and tried to escape. Kelk seized him and the two of them fell, rolling on the ground and scuffling. Bamford's wife called out for him to stop them, and he cleared the wall again, trying to pull them apart. He discovered that 'Burns' was holding a knife, and tugged it out of his hand. Bamford grabbed hold of the man, but 'Burns' again broke free and ran off into the dark, eluding both Bamford and Burnam, who had also come over the wall. Bamford asked his friend to strike a match, and by its light they saw that George Kelk lay bleeding heavily on the ground. They and Nuttall lifted him up and carried him to a house nearly opposite the gates. The knife-wound proved fatal, and Kelk died within minutes of being struck. The ineffectual efforts of Bamford's party, doubtless due in part to their befuddled state, failed to stop the killer getting away, and to make matters worse Bamford himself wiped the blood from the blade of the knife!

George Seath, a chemist, of Lordsmill Street, Chesterfield, was called and examined the body at 10.15 pm, and half an hour later Mr Henry Robinson, surgeon, of Low Pavement, Chesterfield made a similar examination. Both found that the luckless George Kelk had been killed by a stab wound penetrating at least three inches into the right thigh, which had severed the femoral artery, and that death must have followed within a few minutes. It was consistent with the weapon Bamford had seized, a large clasp-knife with a five-inch blade. This, and the cap that the murderer had let fall as he fled, were later produced in evidence. Holmes and others visited the garden, and confirmed that potatoes had recently been removed, comparable with those found on the killer. Meanwhile, confusion continued to reign. By the time the police examined the murder scene, the place was so trampled by curious sight-seers it was impossible to find any other clues.

The culprit, too, was still at large. 'Simon Burns' was the alias of one George Hughes, known locally by the nickname of 'Gorley'. He had worked for a time at Grassmoor Colliery, but seems to have had a semi-nomadic existence, also doing farm labouring on a seasonal basis. For the past four months he had been lodging with Benjamin and Emma Rawson at their house in Winsick, a hamlet in Hasland parish. The couple later testified at the inquest – held on Monday 28 September, in the Municipal Hall – that Hughes had left the house on Saturday morning, returning at 6 am on the Sunday morning. A police officer had visited the house a short time before, so the Rawsons had heard about the killing at Bank Close, and suspected their lodger of the crime. Rawson went so far as to accuse him directly, and on being told that Kelk was dead, Hughes once more began to cry. He then took a cake and half a pound of cheese, and left the house within five minutes of arriving. Rawson, who claimed he was afraid of Hughes, made no effort to stop him, and the fugitive was last seen making towards Calow. Only after he was gone did Rawson start looking for a policeman.

Throughout the inquest, and the later adjourned inquest of Thursday, 1 October, the coroner expressed horrified disbelief at the muddle and ineptitude that had allowed the killer to escape with such ease from a crime scene crowded with witnesses, and the foolishness shown by Bamford in cleaning the murder weapon. Nor was he too impressed by Rawson's behaviour in letting Hughes go unmolested. The inquest jury returned a verdict that George Hughes (alias 'Gorley') was guilty of the wilful murder of George Kelk.

The funeral of George Kelk, ironically the one man to show kindness to Hughes when he was first captured, took place at Hasland churchyard on Wednesday 30 September. There was a large attendance, and as the coffin was lowered 'a profound silence was maintained, only broken by the sobs of sorrowing people around the grave.' The murdered coachman was thirty years old.

As for the much-travelled Hughes, he got as far as South Yorkshire before finally being caught. At 2 am on Friday 2 October, Constable Taylor of the Yorkshire force apprehended the fugitive at Wombwell Main colliery, and Hughes made a partial confession. The Chesterfield police were notified by telegram, and at 6.30 pm on Friday evening he was brought by train to the Midland Railway Station. It was reported that 'a great crowd had collected to see him, and gave utterance to their feelings by groans.'

The twenty-two-year-old Hughes duly came to trial at the

Derby Crown Court on Monday 7 December, where Mr Justice
Byles presided. Faced with a prosecution charge of wilful
murder, defence counsel Vernon Blackburn countered with the
claim that Hughes had lost his way in the dark, that he had
struck out in fear, and had not intended to kill his victim. Given
the defendant's unstable mental state, this was quite a believable
story. Summing up, the judge pointed out to the jury that to take
potatoes from the ground while growing did not constitute a
felony, merely a misdemeanour, and strictly speaking no-one
had the right to try arresting Hughes for so doing. In any case,
it would have been difficult to positively identify the potatoes as
coming from Mr Drabble's garden. Having considered these
facts, the jurors returned a verdict of manslaughter against
Hughes, who was then addressed by Mr Justice Byles. It was the
judge's opinion that the verdict was the right one, and that
Hughes had not meant to kill the luckless Kelk. On the other
hand, there could be no excuse for his using such a fearsome
weapon, however unwittingly, to such deadly effect, and for this
he must be punished. He sentenced Hughes to fifteen years
penal servitude.

Hughes had escaped the gallows by a hair's breadth. All the
same, one short act of violence resulting from foolishness and
terror had cost him dear. His young life was to be blighted by a
long prison sentence, while for George Kelk justice came far too
late. For both men, it was a terrible price to pay for a few stolen
potatoes!

Chapter 14

The Sanguinary Conflict 1870

On the rural areas of North Derbyshire, sheepstealing was a constant problem to local farmers, and to the police officers investigating the thefts. Regarded as a serious crime, it still carried the penalty of a severe prison term, but this did not diminish the activities of the thieves. Usually local men, their knowledge of the country was often better than that of their pursuers, and the threat of prison made them more likely to resist arrest. Efforts to apprehend sheepstealers led to frequent scuffles, and sometimes the violence got out of hand. An incident close to the Cliffe Wheel Dam at Sothall, near Beighton, involved one of the leading figures of the Derbyshire Constabulary, and almost cost him his life.

During the winter of 1869-70, the area around Eckington was hit by a major outbreak of sheepstealing, and the widespread nature of the thefts suggested that the whole operation was being run by an organised gang. The local police did their best to track down the culprits, but up to February 1870 had not had much success.

The officer in charge was Dennis Gorman, Superintendent of

The district of Sothall, now a modern suburb of Beighton, scene of Dennis Gorman's encounter with the sheep-stealer in 1870. Dennis Middleton

the Eckington Division. As a sergeant, Gorman had investigated the Ashover murder in 1857, and although no conviction was secured, he evidently impressed his superiors. In the years that followed he had risen to Inspector at Clay Cross, and after a brief period of service at Chester had returned to take on senior rank in Derbyshire once again. Intelligent, well-read and articulate, devoutly religious, Gorman was also determined and thorough, with a fearless, combative nature. If any fault could be held against him, it was that sometimes he was too brave for his own good. On the morning of Tuesday, 22 February 1870, the butchered carcass of a sheep, whole but for a few missing joints, was found under some bushes near the Cliffe Wheel Dam at Sothall, a hamlet just south of Beighton. This area is now in South Yorkshire, but up until the 1960s was part of Derbyshire, and came within Superintendent Gorman's Eckington Division. On hearing of the discovery, he attended the crime scene in person, accompanied by several other officers. Having studied the ground and the carcass, Gorman decided that the thief would probably be coming back before long to collect his 'kill'. He detailed the other officers to search the area for the poacher or the missing joints of meat, and hid himself in a nearby wood, waiting for his quarry to return.

He had not been waiting long when a powerful, thick-set man emerged from deeper in the wood, and made for the place where the slaughtered sheep was hidden. Unaware he was being watched, the newcomer gathered up the stolen meat, crammed it into a sack and a bundle that he carried, and set off towards Beighton with his illicit burden. Gorman allowed him to get so far, then edged out from cover and followed. Coming up quietly behind the thief, he called out that he should consider himself under arrest on a charge of sheepstealing. Startled by the sudden appearance of the police officer, the man made no resistance. He let the superintendent lead him down towards the road, where Gorman intended to join his fellow officers, but this behaviour was evidently a ruse on his part. By apparently 'coming quietly', the thief caused Gorman to think the arrest was completed, an almost fatal mistake.

Once down on the road, the situation changed. The sheepstealer's hand darted into his coat pocket, and came out gripping a loaded pistol, which he aimed point-blank at Gorman's face. The superintendent lashed out hurriedly with the stick he carried, trying to deflect the weapon, but the trigger was pulled before he could knock it away, and not all of the blast missed its target. The charge of pigeon shot peppered Gorman's left cheek, forehead, neck, shoulder and ear, and the close-range powder-smoke blinded and choked him. Unable to see and struggling to breathe, he managed to grab his attacker and hung grimly on to him, pouring blood from the gunshot wounds he had taken.

A desperate hand-to-hand encounter followed, Gorman grappling bravely with his opponent but gradually weakening from pain and blood loss, while the thief kicked and struck at him, clubbing him over the head with the butt of the empty pistol and then biting like a wild animal at the policeman's fingers and tearing the flesh in his efforts to get free. Faced with the threat of a prison sentence, the man clearly intended to dispose of Gorman as the only living witness to his crime. He drew a clasp-knife, intending to stab the superintendent, who still fought on, fending off the thrusts as best he could. By now Gorman was close to losing consciousness, and there can surely be no doubt that had the fight continued he would have died. Luckily for him, three men drove by in a cart, and caught sight of what the *Derbyshire Times* rightly described as 'the sanguinary conflict' below them. Seeing Gorman being dragged struggling along the ground, and a shocking trail of bloodstains visible for

Sothall outskirts, showing the woodland and shrubbery that would have been more in evidence when Gorman lay in wait for his quarry. Dennis Middleton

several yards on the road, they hurried to the rescue. The sheepstealer was overpowered, and he and the injured policeman were driven back to Eckington.

For a while it was doubtful that Gorman would survive, and for several days he lay delirious and close to death. Three pieces of shot were removed from his face and neck, but as many more remained embedded, causing him pain and discomfort for the rest of his life. The pistol-flash left him blind for a fortnight, and the sight of one eye was affected. He was also suffering from the blows to his head, and bruised all over his body from the kicks and punches of the thief. The doctor in attendance clearly expected him to die, and prevented any attempt to take a statement from him due to his 'dangerous condition'.

Gorman, though, had other ideas. Although badly injured, he eventually recovered to testify, and was present at the trial of his would-be murderer. On Wednesday, 20 July 1870, a thirty-eight-year-old labourer, William Wallinger, was charged with 'shooting, on the 22 February last, with a pistol, at Dennis Gorman, with intent wilfully and with malice aforethought to kill and murder him, at Beighton, near Eckington, Derbyshire.' Found guilty of the attempted murder of a police officer in addition to his earlier crime, Wallinger was sentenced to life imprisonment.

For Superintendent Gorman, too, it was an ending of another kind. The injuries he had suffered meant that he was unable to carry on his duties, and his distinguished police career was brought to a violent close. Commended by the trial judge, who 'did not know how it was possible for any officer to have acted more courageously'(wisely, he forbore to comment on the foolhardy single-handed attempt at arrest for which Gorman had so nearly paid with his life) and awarded him £20. In March 1871 he was also presented with the larger sum of £155 from the Eckington Association for the Prosecution of Felons, who evidently appreciated his work for law and order in their area. But as one door closed, another opened for him, and in 1879 Dennis Gorman became the first Librarian of Chesterfield. It was a post in which he was to serve – again with distinction – for the next thirty years, dying in office in 1909. Though his later career was often stormy, it must have seemed a haven of peace after the bloody encounter by the Cliffe Wheel Dam, so many years before.

Chapter 15

Desperate Encounter with a
Pig-Stealer
1871

Towards the end of 1871, while former Superintendent Gorman was still recovering from the injuries sustained in his battle with the sheepstealer, a remarkably similar struggle took place at Dronfield, only a few miles from Beighton. Once again, the fight was marked by extreme violence, and once more a police officer was involved. This time, though, the would-be thief had come not in search of sheep, but pigs!

In the early hours of Saturday, 11 November 1871, Sergeant Borritt was making what he probably imagined would be a normal routine patrol of the area. As he passed the *Coach and Horses* public house by Birchitt Bar, he heard the squealing of

Coach and Horses, *Birchitt Bar, Dronfield. Here another police officer came close to death in 1871, this time battling with a pig-stealer!* Sue Crabbe

frightened pigs coming from one of the nearby outbuildings, and went to investigate. Peering in through the early morning gloom, Borritt caught sight of a man standing in a corner at the end of the building, and ordered him to come out and be seen. The man did not keep him waiting. Jumping over a low wall, he swung his fist, narrowly missing Borritt's head, and the fight was on.

The sergeant caught hold of his attacker, and 'a struggle of a desperate character commenced'. Borritt's adversary was carrying three butcher's knives and a sharpening steel - a fact that the policeman no doubt discovered by touch as they grappled together - and called out to the sergeant that he would kill rather than be taken alive. Both combatants lost their footing and fell to the ground, still struggling. Then the man broke free, scrambling to his feet, and kicked viciously at Borritt, who was still down. The sergeant was booted in the head and face several times 'with the utmost violence', and could easily have died or lost consciousness at this point. Fortunately he managed to keep his wits about him, and struggled to his feet. His attacker tugged out one of the knives he carried, and stabbed at him, cutting him through the right thumb as Borritt tried to parry the blow.

Realising that this was now a life and death situation, the sergeant used his whistle to summon help, and luckily for him a second officer, Constable Moore, came running in answer. The criminal still fought on, shouting that he would not be taken even by both of them, but now the odds were with the party of law and order. Borritt delivered a heavy blow with his staff that sent his opponent staggering, and the two policemen managed to get the handcuffs on him at last. The butchering tools the offender carried indicated why he was there, and a search of the building where the pigs were kept provided further confirmation. Inside, the officers found a rope of the kind butchers used to tie pigs for slaughter, and the snout of one of the animals showed rope-marks where the would-be thief had tried to drag it out to be killed.

The pigstealer at first refused to give a name, but by the time he came to trial in Derby at the December Assizes he had been identified as John Taylor. The report of the trial described him as 'a rough-looking fellow', which certainly seems to match his behaviour the previous month! Charged with unlawful wounding of a police officer, and intention to commit grievous bodily harm, Taylor was found guilty, and although sentence was initially deferred, it seems reasonable to assume that he eventually served a prison term. Borritt was badly hurt, suffering severe contusions from the kicks he had taken to the head while on the ground, and was still recuperating from his injuries at the time of the trial, but fortunately lived to testify.

Looked at over the passage of a century and more, this particular scuffle now appears almost comical, but there can be no doubt that Taylor meant to carry out his threats. Faced with likely imprisonment, the pigstealer – like William Wallinger before him - aimed to remove the only witness to his crime. Had Borritt not been able to call for help, and had Constable Moore not been there to hear him, the pigsty by the *Coach and Horses* might well have been the scene of another unsolved Derbyshire murder!

Chapter 16

He Did Not Think He Should Recover
1871

A ppearing at the same Derby Assizes as John Taylor in December 1871 was the Chesterfield shoemaker Samuel Wallis. His crime, committed only a few days before the pigstealer's battle with the sergeant, was far more terrible, for Wallis faced a charge of wilful murder.

Samuel Wallis and his wife Sarah lived at Wheatbridge Place, at the end of Boythorpe Lane, which is now part of Chesterfield but was then on the far western edge of the old borough. In fact, the couple's house was situated at the meeting-point of four different parishes – to the east, Chesterfield, to the west Brampton, with Newbold and Hasland lying to north and south. They had two young children, a six-year-old boy and a baby of eighteen months. Until the later part of 1871 the family appeared to be happy, both husband and wife respected by their neighbours as hard-working and honest folk. As the year wore on, however, a darker shadow fell over their lives. Samuel Wallis fell victim to a severe depression, and became convinced that he was in the grip of a fatal illness.

For three months, from September to November 1871, Wallis was a regular visitor to the surgery of Mr Richard Jeffreys at Elder Yard in Chesterfield. The surgeon was later to recall visiting Wallis at his home for several weeks, while Wallis had been coming to the surgery twice a week, obviously very worried. Jeffreys decided that his patient was suffering from 'derangement of the stomach and liver with general debility, defection of spirits, and indisposition to activity', the underlying cause being hypochrondria, 'a disease in which the brain and nervous system are more or less affected'. More disturbingly, indicating Wallis' state of mind, he added of his patient that 'he did not think he should recover.' Mr Jeffreys had suggested that 'a change of air' might be beneficial to his patient, and this seems to have been taken up by Wallis. The family had visited Birmingham the day before, and apparently Mrs Wallis had been saving some of the earnings she made as a dressmaker to arrange a trip to 'somewhere beyond Derby'. Sadly, this excursion was never to take place.

Early in the morning of Wednesday 8 November, the family were in bed at their home in Wheatbridge Place. They slept together in one bed, with six-year-old George lying at the foot of the bed and his parents and baby brother at the top. All at once young George was awoken by what he later described as 'my father pushing my mother at my legs', and gave a startled scream. His father, Samuel Wallis, got out of bed and went downstairs dressed only in his shirt and trousers. The boy thought he saw a knife in his hand. Looking at his mother, George was shocked to see blood pouring from her mouth. She fell away from his legs to one side, and screamed, and he could see more blood on the side of the bed.

Unable to help her, but showing considerable presence of mind for one so young, George picked up his baby brother and left the house by the back door, making for the home of his uncle, Mr Hopkinson. The latter was then at work, but George's grandmother, Mrs Mary Hopkinson, was at home, and listened with horror to the youngster's story, confirmed by the splashes of blood on his face. Returning to the house with another woman, she called out 'Sam', but got no answer, and on entering the bedroom found her daughter lying dead across the bed, with her feet to the floor, as though she had been sitting on the bed. Mrs Hopkinson raised the alarm, and the surgeon Mr Bluett was at the house about 7 am, with Inspector Brady arriving soon after at 7.30 am.

Bluett found Mrs Wallis, dressed in chemise, nightgown and petticoat skirt, lying on her back with her arms by her sides, her feet resting on the floor. The body was still warm, and blood still foamed from the mouth and nostrils. There was more blood on the body itself, and the bedclothes were soaked with it. Examining the dead woman, Bluett discovered a stab wound to the fingers of the left hand, and a more deadly wound three-quarters of an inch long, just below the collar bone, where a

B.M. 275·7

810

Gasometer

CHESTER

813

814

B.M. 296·8

276

281

815

28 FT. R.H.

UPRIGHT

Gas Works

Gasometer

C.8.

B.M. 271·9

WM.
OW.

CHESTER STREET

BURROWS YARD

B.M. 271·8

T

B.M. 268·1

West

S.R.

P.O.Box
274

Mount Zion
Chapel
(Wesleyan)

c.

Brampton
Brewery

P.

Wheat Bridge

32

TAP LANE

B.M. 269·4

WM.o

A.D.

H

B.M. 275·5

OLD

WM.o

F.P.

Weir

c.

FURNACE LANE

COATES'S YARD

Inn

Inn

B.M. 269·7

c.

WS.

Wheatbridge
Mills
(Flint &c.)

Bridge

lma Pottery

T.

273

T.

Weir

270

T.

62

267

Wire and
Needle Works

e

T.

R

i

V

BM. 275·6

B.M. 27

ks

Chemical

Furnacehill

blade of some kind had been thrust home. When he performed the postmortem later on, he was to find that the blade had gone five or six inches under the collar-bone and upwards into the throat, cutting the carotid artery and perforating the windpipe. It appeared that she had been stabbed while in bed, attempted to sit up, and fallen back again. From the warmth of the body and other signs, Bluett did not think she had been dead for more than fifteen minutes.

Inspector Brady was able to confirm the position and wounds of the deceased, and made a search of the rooms. In the bedroom he found leather and a shoemaker's knife, and guessed that Wallis had plied his trade upstairs. He also found a second knife, lying on a piece of carpet and stained with blood on the blade and handle. The murder weapon was a shoemaker's knife with a five-inch blade, worn to a point by long usage. By now the hunt was on for Samuel Wallis, and the Chesterfield police force under Superintendent Oldham scoured the neighbourhood in search of him. Charles Goodwin, a day labourer at Robinson's Pill Box factory in the Wheatbridge area of Brampton, had seen him leave the house 7 am and walk quickly up Boythorpe Lane, but since then there had been no sign of him. Given his state of mind, it seemed likely that he had committed suicide by drowning himself, or throwing himself down one of the numerous coal pit shafts that dotted the industrial landscape of Brampton and Walton to the west of the town. The river was dragged, and collieries searched, but to no avail. It was not until the early hours of Thursday morning that he was run to ground, when around 2 am Inspector Brady himself discovered the killer in a pit cabin belonging to Mr Ludlam, in the Walton area. Although Brady knew Wallis well by sight, he had trouble recognising him at first. Wallis had evidently tried to hide himself up a chimney, and his face and clothes were blackened with soot, giving him a totally strange appearance. Brady had to ask if he was indeed Samuel Wallis, and having received a reply in the affirmative, told his quarry he was under arrest charged with murdering his wife. Wallis, whose outward lack of any emotion certainly suggests a serious psychological disorder, made no resistance, merely enquiring if his wife was really dead. Told that she was,

Wheatbridge Place, in 1871 the meeting-place for four separate Derbyshire parishes. It was where Sarah Wallis came to a violent end. Ordnance Survey Sheet XXV.6 1st ed, 1876, 25″ to 1 mile, Chesterfield Local Studies Library

he replied 'well, it is a bad job'. After some thought, he added that 'she must have put me about very much, and there were knives about.'

Wallis was brought before magistrate E G Maynard at Chesterfield County Police Court later on Thursday, the inquest having been begun and adjourned on Wednesday evening while the search was going on. Mr Bluett, Mrs Hopkinson, Inspector Brady and young George Wallis all appeared and gave evidence, as did surgeon Richard Jeffreys. While there could be no doubt that Wallis had killed his wife, there appeared to be no reason for his actions. By all accounts the couple were very fond of each other, there had been no history of quarrels between them – young George recalled once seeing his mother hit his father in the eye with her elbow, but this could well have been an accidental collision rather than a blow – and the family were far from destitute. The police had taken charge of a bank book and cash to the value of £30, and some sixty pairs of boots and shoes from the business. The sole cause had to be Wallis's own hypochondria and his disturbed mental state. Throughout his court appearance he showed the same lack of emotion as before, 'not seeming to realise his awful position.' Only at the end of the trial did some hint of feeling break through in a moving incident, when George approached Wallis and uttered the word 'father', and the murderer pressed his child 'most affectionately' by the hand. The adjourned inquest resumed on Friday, and the jury returned a verdict of wilful murder. Samuel Wallis was committed for trial at the Derbyshire Winter Assizes. For what he had done, insanity was now his only possible defence.

An unconnected event, reported on the same page as Wallis's own trial, indicates what other random dangers lurked in Chesterfield at that time. Frank Stuart White, son of the wine and spirit merchant J B White, died of the bite of a rabid dog which entered his father's High Street premises on 14 August and attacked his fox terrier. Attempting to part them, young White was badly bitten on the left hand, and for a time seemed to recover, but the full-blown symptoms struck on Monday 6 November. He finally succumbed to 'the convulsive paroxysms peculiar to the disease' at 7 am on Wednesday 8 November, virtually the same time that Mrs Wallis had died. He was twenty-four years old.

Sergeant Watson, who escorted Wallis by train from Chesterfield to the gaol at Derby, gained some insight into the hellish visions plaguing his prisoner. Wallis told the policeman how when he came to Ludlam's colliery 'there was such a fearful thundering noise in the pit I was so glad to get out' and that 'Brampton looked so black and dark' he had crept up the flue to hide. Pointing to the sky, he told Watson 'look at the sky, it looks like Hell fire' and that it was 'as if they were burning brimstone'. In between these tormented outbursts he informed his captor of various arrangements he would like to make, nominating relatives to bring up his children and asking that the money and furniture be taken care of on their behalf. At one point he peered out of the window, and Watson grabbed him, thinking he might jump out, but Wallis told him 'I shall not do that; I am only taking a last look at the old church and the old place.' It was to be his final farewell to the town where he had lived, and for several years worked as a well-liked and respected tradesman.

Mr Justice Lush presided at the Winter Assizes at Derby County Hall on Friday, 16 December, when the thirty-six-year-old Wallis appeared to answer the charge of wilful murder on his wife Sarah Wallis, and pleaded 'not guilty'. Once more the witnesses were called and the facts presented. As before, everyone – including the late woman's mother, Mrs Hopkinson – agreed that the Wallises had been a happy, loving couple and that the one problem had been the mental illness of the past few months. Mr Vernon Blackburn, the defence counsel, pleaded that Wallis had killed his wife while suffering from 'homicidal mania', and was not responsible for his actions. The lack of any motive for murder, and confirmatory comments by medical experts on the state of the prisoner's mind, favoured this line of defence. Mr Justice Lush was not convinced, and when summing up expressed the view that the evidence had not proved the prisoner to be insane. It was up to the jury to decide if they thought Wallis had been 'seized by a fit of frenzy, which left him no longer a free agent.' If they did not, they must return a verdict of wilful murder, as there was no indication that Sarah had given her husband any cause for such a brutal act.

The jury foreman seemed a little confused himself, and at first gave a verdict of 'not guilty', but immediately corrected himself and answered 'guilty'. The judge donned the black cap, at which the foreman added that the jury recommended mercy for Wallis 'on account of his previous weakness.' Mr Justice Lush addressed the prisoner and pronounced the death sentence, which Wallis, although looking pale and ill, heard 'apparently unmoved'. Although he had been sentenced to hang, the feeling in the court was that the punishment would not be carried out.

Nor was it. The Home Secretary approved the jury's recommendation, and Wallis was reprieved ('respited', in the jargon of the day). His hanging, set for Friday, 29 December, was cancelled, and he was to be held in confinement at Broadmoor. News of the decision was received by Wallis with the same lack of emotion, and the *Derbyshire Times* of 30 December 1871 decided that 'there has been nothing in his behaviour since his condemnation of any importance.'

Sunk in the terrible prison of his own deranged mind, one suspects that Samuel Wallis no longer cared whether he lived or died.

Chapter 17

She Had Drink Every Day
1872

A year after the Wallis murder case, another household in the Chesterfield area witnessed a violent death. The scene was Wellington Street, New Whittington, and the participants John and Selina Bennett. Bennett worked as a miner at a neighbouring colliery, and he and his forty-six-year-old wife were a very different couple from Samuel and Sarah Wallis. Throughout their marriage, it was claimed that they had lived together 'most unhappily' and their home was a setting for frequent quarrels. The main problem for the Bennetts was not the scourge of insanity, but that of drink and domestic violence. It was the view of those who knew them that Selina was a heavy drinker, who according to one neighbour 'had drink every day' and was often encountered in a drunken state. Her addiction to alcohol only served to rouse the violent temper of her husband, and on more than one occasion he had struck his wife.

Wellington Street, New Whittington, the location for the brutal killing of Selina Bennett by her husband John. Dennis Middleton

On the morning of Monday, 11 November, about 9.40 am, the Bennetts' next-door neighbour, Mrs Hannah Allton, called on Mrs Bennett to find her locking the door of her house. Mrs Bennett told the other woman she was going to the *Wellington* public house to bring back her husband. Not for the first time, Mrs Allton noted she was not sober. She heard Mrs Bennett return shortly before 10.30 at night, but did not hear John Bennett come in. Soon afterwards the couple could be heard arguing for up to three-quarters of an hour. Mrs. Allton, who was in bed with her book-keeper husband William Allton, was startled to hear a shout, and the noise of a heavy fall. Concerned at first, she did not pay too much attention to it, as the Bennetts were well known for their quarrels, but she was sure it must have been Mrs Bennett who fell, and hers the voice that cried out. She recalled that 'John Bennett's voice was very loud', but soon afterwards sleep overcame her, and she heard nothing more.

The following morning Mrs Allton heard someone knocking on her wall from next door. Her husband went round to the house, and found Selina Bennett lying on the couch, looking very ill. He sent for his wife, who saw that her neighbour's left eye was blackened, and the left side of her face badly swollen as if from a blow. Mrs Bennett told Mrs Allton she was sick from a fall, and that her husband had caused it with 'a kick in her bowels.' She (Bennett) complained of pain in her 'bowels', the area of her groin and lower abdomen. Worried and angry at what she had seen, Mrs Allton confronted Bennett when he came home. She rebuked him for the treatment of his wife, telling him there were better ways of solving a problem than 'giving black eyes', a charge to which he made no answer. Questioned by Mr Allton as to the injuries to Selina's body, Bennett claimed these had been caused by his wife running away from him after he had struck her, and falling over a bucket. He admitted to Allton that he had struck his wife in the face on previous occasions 'to shame her' for her heavy drinking.

Whatever the cause, Selina Bennett's condition rapidly worsened, and on Tuesday, 19 November a surgeon, Mr T F Hale, was called from the adjoining village of Barrow Hill. On arriving at the house, he found Mrs Bennett in bed and suffering severe pain from a hugely distended abdomen. Hale noted two black eyes, one of which also showed injury to the superior maxillary bone, but the main damage was internal, and his patient's complaint was of 'intense pain in the lower part of her person'. In spite of all Mr Hale's efforts, Selina Bennett was beyond help. She lingered in great pain for the next three days, finally dying on Friday, 22 November. Hale's postmortem examination two days later found severe injuries to the bone of the eye, and the colouring suggested that the blows had been struck on separate occasions roughly a week apart. On the right groin he found an abrasion an inch and a half long and half an inch wide, now scabbed over. The dead woman's vagina had a laceration of three-quarters of an inch long by half an inch deep near the left side of the opening of the urethra. An internal examination revealed evidence of severe inflammation and congestion of the stomach, and also showed the destructive effects of Selina's alcoholism. The liver crumbled in Hale's fingers, and the gall bladder contained forty-seven calculi, and the spleen was congested. Selina Bennett was clearly a sick woman, but in spite of the self-inflicted damage of her drinking, and the rapid decomposition of the corpse which made his task both difficult and unpleasant, Hale's examination confirmed his initial diagnosis that death had resulted from exhaustion following peritonitis, which could have been caused by 'disease or ill usage'. He emphasised the fact that the injuries must have been 'the result of very considerable violence.'

An inquest was held on Saturday, 23 November at the *Forge Inn*, New Whittington, where Hale testified, and following an adjournment was resumed at the same venue the following Tuesday, where Mr and Mrs Allton gave their account of the recent events. The quarrelsome nature of the couple's marriage, and Bennett's past violence, were both demonstrated, as was the dead woman's addiction to the bottle. Their son, Edwin, had apparently left home because of their arguments, while Mrs Allton testified that on Tuesday morning she had seen Selina take 'one quartern of gin', and that while Bennett was rarely drunk his wife 'had drink every day (gin and beer mixed)'. Mr Hale gave the findings of his post-mortem examination, and while admitting the low state of Selina's health, expressed the firm opinion that she had not died from natural causes. Death was due to 'exhaustion following acute peritonitis, in connection with the injury over the pubis, and the laceration of the vagina.' The peritonitis, he claimed, was caused by 'injury to the lower part of the person which I fancy was done by one blow. Those injuries arose from violence such as might follow a kick.' There was no possibility that Selina could have injured herself in such a way by falling on a bucket. Edwin Bennett having identified the body of his mother, the coroner's jury returned a verdict of manslaughter against John Bennett, who was committed for trial on the Coroner's warrant.

Bennett appeared before Mr Justice Denman at the Derbyshire Spring Assizes on Friday, 14 March 1873, charged with 'killing and slaying' his wife. Mr Weightman prosecuted, while Mr Vernon Blackburn acted as defence counsel. The evidence of the witnesses was repeated, recounting the events leading up to Selina's death, and the couple's unhappy marriage. The results of Hale's examination were heard, together with his conclusion that a kick was the likely cause of death. The defence trotted out the old, discredited bucket story, and more tellingly referred to Selina's 'intemperate habits' and the fact that she had suffered the injuries while intoxicated. Perhaps the strongest argument mustered by Mr Blackburn was that 'there were evidences that inflammation of the bowels might have resulted without violence being used.' He must have presented a persuasive case, as the jury felt unable (or unwilling) to convict John Bennett of manslaughter. Amazingly, and against the medical evidence, he was acquitted of the charge.

When Selina Bennett died, she was destroying herself with alcohol. Nowadays she would be seen to be suffering from an illness, and have the option of Alcoholics Anonymous, and rehabilitation. Instead, in 1872 she provoked the violent temper of her husband, with fatal results. There is no doubt that John Bennett was sorely tried by his wife's drinking, and in all likelihood he had no intention of killing her, but one cannot help but feel that he was fortunate to escape the charge of manslaughter.

Perhaps the jury felt that he had already suffered enough.

Chapter 18

A Doctor in the Dock
1873

Young Louisa Atkin was pregnant. By December 1872 her mother, Eliza, had noted the familiar signs and in spite of her daughter's denials had, as she put it, 'observed that she was in the family way.' Ordinarily this might have been the cause of rejoicing and celebration, but Mrs Atkin's discovery was anything but a pleasant surprise. Her daughter, who was only sixteen years of age, lived with her parents and their six other children in the village of Biggin, in the Peak District of Derbyshire, and was as yet unmarried.

Among the Victorians, sex before marriage, though often indulged in covertly, was rarely admitted in public. The pregnancy of young unmarried girls was seen as a disgrace, and carried a lasting stigma not only to the person involved but to all her family. If such an 'unfortunate accident' could be concealed, even by the risky process of abortion, this was preferable to the humiliation of it being public knowledge. In a time when large numbers of women died from the complications of childbirth, this way of thinking all too often led to sickness and premature death.

Appalled by the likely consequences for their sixteen-year-old daughter and themselves, Mrs Atkin and her farmer husband William decided that the pregnancy would have to be terminated. Her husband had another, darker reason to conceal the forthcoming birth. William Atkin, it seems, had enjoyed incestuous sex with his daughter, and was the father of her child.

Biggin, where the Atkins lived, lies near Hartington in the north-west of Derbyshire, not far from the Staffordshire border, and is not to be confused with the village of the same name in the vicinity of Wirksworth, where James Haliburton committed his rape in 1786. It was from the neighbouring Staffordshire village of Longnor that the Atkins sought medical assistance now, rather than risk calling on the services of their local doctor Mr Thomas Twigg. By 11 February 1873 the evidence of Louisa's condition was too obvious to be denied, and she admitted to her mother that she was indeed expecting a child, and delivered the shocking news that William Atkin was the father. That same day, 'at the request of her husband', Mrs Atkin made the journey to Longnor and called on Dr James Poole, who practised in the village. It seems that Poole was not entirely respectable in the eyes of some of his medical colleagues, and in addition to his normal medical practice was known as an 'accoucheur' or abortionist, who might be persuaded to terminate awkward pregnancies. This was certainly in the mind of Mrs Atkin, who delivered her husband's request that Poole provide her with 'some medicine' for the purpose. Realising the situation, Dr Poole enquired how far advanced the pregnancy was, and on being told it was some three or four months replied that it was already too late for medicine to be effective. However, he could use a surgical instrument which would 'put her to rights'.

At this point Mrs Atkin grew worried, and expressed her fear that such an operation could prove dangerous. Poole dismissed her worries, telling her there was nothing to worry about, and that he was willing to perform the service for only £1. Still troubled, but aware that she was under orders from her guilty husband, Mrs Atkin agreed, and Poole travelled back with her in the carrier's cart to the house that evening.

He arrived at 8 pm, carrying a case of surgical instruments from which he selected an unpleasant-sounding item which the girl's mother described as 'a silver tube' with a turn at the end. Louisa having been confined to bed, Poole departed for the bedroom, assuring Mrs Atkin he would be only a few minutes. Half an hour later he was still upstairs, and the mother began to suspect that something was wrong. She called out, asking him why he was taking so long, and Poole replied that he would be down shortly. In fact ten minutes had elapsed before he returned, and he would have left the house without saying

ALFRED LOWE,
(LATE HEYWOOD,)
DISPENSING & FAMILY CHEMIST,
MARKET HALL, CHESTERFIELD.

GENUINE PATENT MEDICINES.

HOMŒOPATHIC MEDICINES.

TOILET SOAPS, TOOTH AND NAIL BRUSHES, POMADES.

HAIR WASHES AND RESTORERS.

COSMETICS and CHOICE PERFUMES in GREAT VARIETY.

Horse & Cattle Medicines of every Description.

AGENT FOR COOPER'S, MC'DOUGALL'S, & BIGG'S SHEEP DIPPING COMPOSITIONS.

LONG'S SPECIFIC, DOWN'S FARMER'S FRIEND, CALVERT'S AND BEACH'S CATTLE FOOD, &c.

OILS, PAINTS, COLOURS, AND VARNISHES.

TURNIP SEEDS, GARDEN SEEDS, ARTIFICIAL TILLAGES, &c.

ALFRED CUPIT,
CHEMIST AND DRUGGIST,
BRAMPTON.

GENUINE PATENT MEDICINES.

Dealer in Petroleum, Paraffin, Benzoline, Paraffin and Benzoline Lamps, Glasses, Wicks, &c.

HORSE & CATTLE MEDICINES.

Agent for HORNIMAN'S PURE TEA.

Advertisements by local chemists in T P Wood's Almanac of 1873, *showing the range of services and items offered. This lax climate enabled doctors such as James Poole to operate as illegal abortionists or accoucheurs.* Chesterfield Local Studies Library

anything had Mrs Atkin not demanded to know if he had been successful. To this Poole replied that 'it was doubtful', but that if the aborted child was not 'discharged' they should contact him.

Once he had gone, Louisa's condition worsened rapidly, and three days later on Friday, 14 February, the desperate William Atkin wrote an undated, unsigned letter to the doctor informing him that there was no change for the better, and imploring him to make a second visit either on Saturday or Monday at the latest, specifying that he should come at night. This shifty missive was later found in Poole's possession after his arrest.

He did not return to the house until the following Monday night, when Mrs Atkin – by now very concerned for her daughter – asked him again if there was any danger in the operation, and told him that if there was, she would rather he did not use the surgical instrument again. To this Poole replied that it was perfectly safe, and that this time he would use a stronger instrument which should do the work. Not long afterwards he came out of the bedroom and told the couple 'he thought it would be all right', but left them a draught of medicine which they were to give Louisa to deaden the pain she was now suffering.

On the night of 18 February, between 9 pm and 10 pm, the young girl became very ill, and grew worse by 11 am the following morning. In accordance with Poole's instructions, her mother gave her some of the medicine, and an hour later Louisa gave birth to a stillborn child. Mrs Atkin, who must have been almost as wretched herself, was present at the birth. William Atkin dug a hole in the garden behind the house, and his wife buried the dead child and covered it with earth. At her frantic urgings, William Atkin went to Longnor in an effort to bring Poole to the house, but the doctor did not return with him. Louisa continued in a sick, delirious state until the morning of Thursday, 20 February, when at 3 am death put an end to her suffering.

Poole, who did not arrive until after she had died, examined her body and informed the parents that death was due to peritonitis. According to one statement by Mrs Atkin, he promised to let them have a death certificate later, but subsequently she was to claim that he had told her there would be no need for an inquest.

In spite of the couple's efforts to keep the matter secret, suspicions were soon aroused. James Poole, it seems, was his own worst enemy in this regard. As early as 11 February he had been seen drinking at the *Devonshire Arms* in Hartington, and boasting that he had attended one of Thomas Twigg's patients, and 'had got a sovereign for it.' Hearing of Louisa's sudden death, Constable John Clarke made a visit to the house, on that day, and when questioned, Mrs Atkin told him what had happened and where the child was buried. The body of the dead child, a baby girl, was recovered, and the day after, on Friday, 21 February an inquest was held, where the girl's mother made a formal statement, accusing her husband of fathering Louisa's child, and of forcing her to go to procure an abortion from Dr Poole. Mrs Atkin claimed she had not wished to go, and did so only 'under fear of her life' from her husband. The jury duly returned a verdict of manslaughter on Poole, who was arrested at midnight on Friday, 21 February by Constable Clarke on the coroner's warrant, and held in readiness to appear at the Ashbourne Petty Sessions the following week. In the course of the arrest, Clarke found the incriminating letter from William Atkin in the doctor's possession. The day before, Parwich surgeon Thomas Nathaniel Twigg carried out a post-mortem examination on Louisa, and was to give damning evidence in his own court appearances.

On Monday, 3 March, James Poole was brought before Sir Percival Heywood and fellow magistrates at the Ashbourne Petty Sessions to answer the charge of manslaughter brought by the coroner's jury. Superintendent Wheeldon of the Derbyshire Constabulary prosecuted, while Mr Tennant, a Staffordshire solicitor, defended the prisoner. Poole's demeanour, both here and afterwards, struck many onlookers as remarkably offhand and nonchalant. He pleaded not guilty to the charge. Mrs Atkin once more gave evidence, as did her sister Ellen Dawson, who had helped look after Louisa in her last hours, and the Hartington saddler William Stone reported seeing Poole in the *Devonshire Arms* and hearing his seemingly incriminating remarks. Mr Twigg, the surgeon, gave the findings of his post-mortem examination, which had revealed that 'the womb was in a gangrenous condition, and the ventricles were contracted. The cause of death, in his opinion, was inflammation of the womb', and could not have been caused by normal childbirth. He strongly condemned the damage done by the instruments Poole had used on the girl, which he ought not to have made use of 'under any circumstances'. As the Atkins' regular doctor, and no doubt stung by Poole's behaviour and his comments in the public house, Mr Twigg probably let a little personal feeling show in his own remark that: 'It was not a suitable instrument, and one which was never used by any gentle man in the medical profession.' It was clear he regarded Poole, who elsewhere is referred to as 'not a regularly qualified doctor' as something of a charlatan. This said, there was no doubt about his findings, which were fully corroborated by the Ashbourne surgeon Mr J Casson.

The medical evidence presented made matters much worse for James Poole. Having used an instrument with the illegal intent of procuring abortion, he was no longer guilty of manslaughter, but now stood accused of wilful murder, with the threat of a capital sentence. Advised by Mr Tennant to reserve his defence, he was sent for trial at the Derbyshire Spring Assizes later that month. In the meantime word of the terrible events had got round the village, and the local people directed their anger at William Atkin. The incestuous seducer found himself besieged in his own house by jeering, hooting crowds, who made their feelings all too clear, and would no doubt have lynched him had he ventured outside. His figure was burned in effigy, and by the time the Assizes were held William Atkin had seized a rare chance to escape and fled the village and his family. No doubt he hoped to find some safer place where his infamy was unknown, but one suspects that it followed him for the rest of his life.

James Poole appeared before Mr Justice Denman at the

Spring Assizes on Friday 14 March, where he was indicted on the charge of wilful murder. The witnesses once more recounted their evidence, the most crucial testimony coming from Mrs Atkin, who under cross-examination admitted that she had previously given a false statement at the inquest, having been told what to say by her husband after he had consulted Poole. It seemed that Poole had not refused to provide a death certificate for the inquest, but told the couple there would be no inquest, and stalled on providing the document. Mrs Atkin further admitted that Louisa had gone to Youlgreave for 'some medicine' two months before Poole was sent for, and that when Mrs Atkin brought the doctor to Biggin she herself was still not absolutely sure her daughter was pregnant, and 'wanted to know her real condition and whether she could be restored to her usual health.'

These admissions did not alter the medical evidence, nor the fact that William Atkin and Poole were the pair most at fault, but they could not help but undermine the case against the doctor. Mrs Atkin had on her own admission lied under oath, which effectively cast doubt on everything she said. In defence of Poole, who once again preserved his easy, unflustered manner in court, his solicitor Mr Waddy presented him as a medical man on an errand of mercy, attending at the request of Mrs Atkin 'for a perfectly innocent purpose', trying to ascertain whether or not Louisa was with child and seeking to put her parents' minds at rest, rather than on a secretive mission of illegal abortion. The letter from Atkin he dismissed. Poole had handed it over at once to the police officer, and told him who it was from, making no attempt to conceal it. In his view it incriminated, not the doctor, but Atkin, 'who had every reason to keep the condition of his child a secret.' He also seized on the admission that 'medicine' had been obtained and used before Poole's visit, and implied that this had contributed to Louisa's ill health and eventual death. Poole, he claimed, had concealed nothing, and was innocent of the charge.

By going back on some parts of her original story, Mrs Atkin had wrecked the case for the prosecution. The jury returned a verdict of 'not guilty' to the charge of murder, and James Poole was acquitted. The events of February and March 1873 saw Mrs Atkin lose her good name, a beloved daughter, and her husband, leaving her alone to provide for her other six children. Louisa Atkin had suffered the shame of incest, suffering which hardly bears thinking about, and eventual death, together with her stillborn child. William Atkin, rightly regarded by most as the 'villain of the piece', was forced to flee the home where he had unleashed his destructive sexual urges. James Poole, accoucheur, guilty of two botched and ultimately fatal operations, was surely the most fortunate of them all. He escaped not merely the rope, but any other charge, and was free to return to his practice in Longnor.

One wonders how often his terrible 'instruments' were used in later years.

Chapter 19

I Have Ended the Job
1873

As has been seen in the case of John and Selina Bennett, domestic violence was very much a part of Victorian life. Beating and abuse of wives and sexual partners features heavily in newspaper reports of the period, and is often a factor in nineteenth-century murders. When to domestic violence one adds personal jealousy, the results can be lethal, and both of these came together in the case of Benjamin Hudson and his wife Elizabeth.

Hudson was a collier, and he and his wife were both in their twenties. The couple, who had two young children, lived first at Handley, and later at the hamlet of Lightwood, both in the old parish of Staveley north-east of Chesterfield, and had been married for two or three years. They had lived together for some time before their marriage. As well as being Hudson's wife,

West Handley, in Staveley parish, starting-point of Elizabeth Hudson's fatal journey in 1873. Dennis Middleton

Elizabeth was also his cousin, and some of their family relationships strike one as unhealthily close. According to the testimony of their neighbours, the couple's life together was unhappy, and marred by violent quarrels.

The root of the problem seems to have been Elizabeth's promiscuity. Prior to taking up with Hudson, she had enjoyed the attentions of two other lovers, a man called James Hibbert, and William Holmes, both of whom still lived in the village. The fact that Holmes was also her uncle added an incestuous element to the situation. Elizabeth had borne an illegitimate child by each of them, before doing the same with Hudson, her eventual husband. While the relationship with Holmes appeared to have ended, Hibbert was still her lover, visiting her openly.

By 1873 the marriage had reached breaking point. Benjamin Hudson was out of work, and Elizabeth was incurring debts with local shopkeepers and leaving him to pay the bills. A violent assault on his wife the previous year had cost Hudson three months in prison, and although bound over to keep the peace for the next six months he soon repeated the offence. On Easter Monday, 13 April 1873 Elizabeth had left her husband to return to her father's house, and another summons against Hudson was settled out of court by his agreeing to a separation, and undertaking to pay five shillings a week as maintenance. He clearly did so under duress, and continued to regard himself as Elizabeth's husband. Matters were made worse by James Hibbert, who was seen to visit Elizabeth again, and who allegedly taunted Hudson by offering him a sovereign for his wife, no doubt hinting at her promiscuity.

On Wednesday 23 April Hudson visited the house of John Morton, a miner, in Lightwood. The two men walked to West Handley, and back again to Lightwood, and during their conversation Hudson 'spoke about his wife keeping company with other men, and said the man she had lived with before (Hibbert) had offered him a sovereign for her.' He said he should not let him or anyone else have her, adding that if he (Morton) would let him have a gun 'he would shoot her and the old bugger as well.' Morton cautioned him to do no such thing. Morton later testified that on another occasion he had spoken to

Hibbert, who had told him (Morton) he would see Elizabeth and 'was going to fetch her' from the house. That same day another local man, James Evans, met Hudson and advised him to get a job and return to his wife, to which the latter replied that he would not get work and would not live with Elizabeth again. Wednesday was also the day on which Emily Cobb of Lightwood asked Mrs Hudson about two unpaid bills, having been directed there by Hudson himself. Elizabeth refused to pay them.

On Thursday 24 April Elizabeth Hudson left her father's house at Handley and went to Lightwood. Hudson's goods had been sold up on Easter Monday, and Elizabeth was to wash out the family home on behalf of former neighbour Mrs Hardwick. She was there all day, and for much of the time Benjamin Hudson was seen loitering in the vicinity, and was heard to use threatening language to her. James Evans saw him in his garden, as did Emily Cobb. She had already spoken to Elizabeth again about the bills, and reported to Hudson. His response was that Elizabeth must pay them herself. Hudson left about 7 pm, claiming he was going to the *George Inn*. His wife left shortly afterwards, and was seen walking in the direction of Handley. Between 7 pm and 8 pm Mrs Hudson was met by Elizabeth Cole, who was walking from Middle Handley to Lightwood. Mrs Hudson expressed fear for her safety, and Elizabeth Cole walked back with her for about 300 yards towards West Handley, then left her. She saw no sign of Benjamin Hudson. She was the last person to see Elizabeth Hudson alive.

Meanwhile, at 7.30 pm that evening, a shoemaker called George Gosling met Benjamin Hudson on the road midway between Middle and West Handley. Gosling asked Hudson what he was doing there, and the latter told him he was going to look for work. Gosling replied that he was wasting his time, as 'they were all filled up'. He and Hudson walked together along the footpath known as Bowman Lane, as far as a stile near Middle Handley, before parting company. On his return later that evening, Gosling was to encounter something far more unpleasant.

Elizabeth Hudson must also have been walking along Bowman Lane in the direction of West Handley. Some time

The entrance to Bowman Lane, Handley, where Mrs Hudson was savagely murdered. Dennis Middleton

prior to 8 pm, close to that same stile, she was attacked and viciously battered to death with an oaken hedge-stake.

It was George Gosling, the West Handley shoemaker, who had the misfortune to discover the body. Returning along Bowman Lane about 9.30 pm, he reached the stile to see a hammer and a broken bottle lying on the ground on its far side. Looking more closely, Gosling made out the prone figure of a girl or woman in the narrow field beyond, her feet towards the stile. He hurried off and told Charles Evans, who returned with him to the spot. Once over the stile, they found the lifeless body of a woman, her face covered with blood. Beside her was an oaken hedge-stake, broken in several places and splattered with blood. Gosling and Evans, with other helpers, carried the body to the

Devonshire Arms at Middle Handley, and notified the police.

Constable Hookin, arriving to study the murder scene, confirmed finding the hedge-stake broken into four pieces, all splashed with blood. Two hairs clung to the largest fragment. Like Gosling and Evans, Hookin saw shards of an earthenware bottle and a pick-hammer lying nearby. Investigating further, he discovered two teeth near a hollow in the earth, a hollow which appeared to have been made by the victim's head being pounded against the ground, clear evidence of the ferocity of the attack. Teeth were missing from the dead woman's mouth, and her face was 'very much cut'.

This proved to be an understatement. Mr Josiah Court, the Staveley surgeon, who examined the corpse the following day, testified that the victim – now known to be Elizabeth Hudson – had seven wounds on her face. One, more terrible than the rest, extended from the right side of the nose to the right ear; it was three inches long and three and a half inches wide, and had broken her cheek-bone, which lay loose in the wound. The windpipe was broken, as was the lower jaw in two places, and the temple artery was cut across. He concluded that at least four blows had been struck, consistent with the hedge-stake produced, and these were the cause of death. A miner, William Robinson, was later to testify that he had repaired the fence near the stile earlier in 1873, and that on 26 April he noticed that one of the hedge-stakes was missing; he remembered it had been there a few days before. It was the same kind of stake as the murder weapon.

The killer was not hard to find, or to convict. Soon after the murder, Benjamin Hudson visited his uncle John Hudson and other neighbours in West Handley, telling them that he had killed Elizabeth and intended to hang himself. His clothes and hands splashed with blood, he arrived at Benjamin Coupe's house, and when the latter mentioned that a hammer had been found Hudson replied that he hadn't used it, but had 'killed the bitch with a hedge stake'. He was attempting to wash off the blood when Constable Hookin arrived and placed him under arrest. Questioned as to what he had done, he answered 'I have ended the job.' He was later to claim that he had met his wife unexpectedly, and killed her in a rage when a fierce quarrel erupted on the subject of their children and the unpaid bills.

On Tuesday 3 May Benjamin Hudson was brought before Magistrate Alfred Barnes at the Municipal Hall in Chesterfield, and charged with the murder of his wife Elizabeth. It was thought that he would arrive the previous day, but his court appearance was delayed, and the crowd that turned up in the rain on Monday had to go away disappointed. In fact he was brought by train as far as Clay Cross, where he was taken by cab to Chesterfield, thus avoiding a possible uproar at the Midland Station. Evidence was heard from a large number of witnesses, and Hudson was committed to the Assizes at Derby. There once more witnesses gave evidence. These included Richard Hudson, cousin to Benjamin and brother to Elizabeth, who recalled talking to the killer and a man named Crofts at Richard's beer-house on Easter Monday. Crofts urged Benjamin Hudson to go and live with his wife, and Hudson had replied that he would not live with her and that 'he should do something to be talked about.' The defence argued for a manslaughter verdict, pointing out that Hudson had not carried any weapon when he met his wife, and stressing Elizabeth's infidelity, but for such a vicious and apparently unprovoked attack there was no excuse.

The jury returned a verdict of wilful murder, but recommended mercy. The judge donned the black cap and sentenced Hudson to death, while promising to forward their recommendation. Hudson heard the sentence with apparent calm, and the court was hushed. The most emotional response came from the judge himself, who 'was affected to tears, and frequently sobbed as he was passing sentence.'

One last pitiful discovery had been made; on the body of the murdered woman a packet of pins was found, with a piece of paper with the verse:

It is not these pins I mean to burn,
But Ben Hudson's heart I mean to turn.
May he neither eat, speak, drink, nor comfort find,
Till he comes to me and speaks his mind.

Once, it would seem, Hudson and his wife had been in love, and

Devonshire Arms, *Middle Handley, the destination Elizabeth Hudson failed to reach.* Dennis Middleton

perhaps something of that feeling remained. Sadly, their passion had proved all too destructive a force, that was to take both their lives.

Hudson was lodged at Derby gaol to await execution, and during his last days had his spiritual needs addressed by two clergyman, the prison chaplain Reverend H Moore, and the High Sheriff's chaplain Reverend A Olivier. Questioned by the latter if he was sorry for what he had done, Hudson replied that he was. 'Is your sorrow on your wife's account or because you have offended God?' Reverend Olivier asked, and Hudson replied 'both'. He attended every divine service held prior to his execution, and on returning from the last of these to the condemned cell, asked a warder, Mr Holmes, to write out the words of the hymn 'Just as I am, without one plea /But that Thy blood was shed for me' which he had just heard sung, and which had evidently made an impression on him. He then sang another Methodist hymn which began: 'We will face the storm, it won't be long, /And anchor by and by.' In a strange way, these last religious musings echo the superstitious verse and the packet of 'charms' on the body of his wife. Several relatives applied to see him, but he expressed no desire to meet them, and they were not admitted. Neither was the 'respectable lady residing in Derby' who came to the gaol to tell the chaplain that it was 'borne in upon her by the Spirit' that she should see Hudson, as she knew how to 'unlock the hearts of men'. Hudson, however did agree to receive a bouquet of flowers from his aunt, and this he took with him to the scaffold.

Benjamin Hudson went to his death on Monday, 4 August 1873. His was the first private execution to take place at Derby, and he was the first Derbyshire murderer to die hidden from the public gaze. When the trap was sprung and he made the two and a half foot drop, Hudson was holding the bouquet in one hand and his cap in the other. Though his neck was broken immediately, convulsive movements continued for up to ten minutes afterwards. The bouquet fell to the ground, but the cap remained clenched in his left hand. Outside the gaol, a crowd of some 200 people heard the crash as the drop fell, and saw the black flag raised. Benjamin Hudson had paid the price for his crime.

Chapter 20

If I Don't Have Her
1873

The area known as Nether Loads lies near to Holymoorside, west of Chesterfield, and once formed part of the large parish of Brampton. A landscape of fields and farms, it has a pleasant rural aspect, but in its time Loads, too, has seen murder done. Less than a fortnight after Benjamin Hudson battered his wife to death at Handley, two more lives were cut short in this idyllic setting. And once more jealousy was at the heart of it all.

William Kitchen Turner lived with his seventy-year-old widowed mother Ann Turner, at the family farm in Nether Loads. Since the death of his father William had worked the farm on her behalf. Although thirty-six years old, he is described as 'a man not quite clear in his intellect', and a hard drinker, a habit which 'aggravated the mental weakness from which he suffered.' Apart from his drinking, William had been no trouble to his mother or anyone else until January 1873, when Sarah Carter was hired by Mrs Turner as a domestic servant.

Sarah was a young girl, only nineteen, and quickly aroused the interest of her employer's son. William Turner may not have been too bright, but he was capable of strong and passionate feelings, and immediately made it clear to Sarah that he found her attractive. According to his mother, their courtship began in the first week Sarah was with them. The two of them continued to enjoy a close relationship, marred by occasional quarrels, for several weeks, but this situation was not to last. Early in April, Sarah Carter met and became friendly with a young militiaman, who had previously courted her sister Hannah.

On Tuesday 22 April Sarah visited Chesterfield to have herself measured for a new pair of boots, and on her return informed Mrs Turner that she had stolen her sister's sweetheart, and that she and Hannah had quarrelled over it. Sarah claimed that the militiaman had proposed marriage to her 'if she would stick with

The rustic landscape of Loads, west of Holymoorside, still farming country today, as it was when the vengeful William Turner strangled Sarah Carter before hanging himself in 1873. Dennis Middleton

him', and that she had accepted his offer. During the same month William came and sat by Sarah in the cowshed while she was milking. Hannah, who was there as a visitor, said that Sarah told him not to think of her any more, as she had 'got another young man'. William asked Sarah if this was true, and she told him it was. At this William got up angrily and went back to the house. He and Sarah had a further quarrel when she told him she intended to 'keep company' with the militiaman.

The following week, on Tuesday, 29 April, Sarah made another visit to Chesterfield. Her story was that she had failed to be measured for her boots the last time, as the bootmaker was not at home. This may have been true, but the fact that the Chesterfield Militia had its barracks just off the Market Place on Vicar Lane, and that they drilled regularly at the edge of town, seems likely to have affected her decision. When she came back, Mrs Turner asked if she had spoken to her prospective husband, and Sarah claimed she had not, but had watched him with his comrades on the militia drill field. Six days later, on Monday, 5 May, she confided in the older woman that she had received a letter from her lover, asking her to meet him the following Sunday evening in Somerset Fields, just east of the borough in the district of Hady. Soon afterwards, when William had joined them, Mrs Turner told him of this latest development. He promptly flew into a rage, and told Sarah 'you shall not go; I'll have you myself.' After he had calmed down and left, Sarah told Mrs Turner that she would 'keep in' with him, so as not to antagonise him again.

By Wednesday, 7 May, it seemed that William's angry outburst was forgotten, and Sarah felt safe enough to tell the widow that he would leave her alone now. William, though, had not forgotten, nor had his feelings changed. As he and his mother ate their dinner together, he told Mrs Turner that 'I ought to have been married long ago. I should have been a better man.' More disturbingly, he remarked 'if I don't have her I'll take care no one else shall have her, and I'll finish myself after.' After he had gone, Sarah came in, and Mrs Turner, by now thoroughly alarmed and concerned for the younger woman, asked what she would do now, as 'he says he will have you, and you say he shall not.' Sarah, though, was undaunted. 'He may say what he likes', she told her employer. 'I am going to have the militiaman.'

Given the choice, it is not too difficult to see why Sarah – a young and presumably attractive girl – should prefer a glamorous militiaman of a similar age to herself, rather than the rough, homespun William who was seventeen years older. Convinced that William had no intention of carrying out his threats, she decided to ignore him. She was wrong.

At about 2 pm that same day William and Sarah went out together on the nearby moors to gather sticks for firewood. It was something they had often done before, and no doubt Sarah felt that by going along with him she would help to avoid any more angry outbursts. Once they had left, neither Mrs Turner nor anyone else was to see them alive again. As the darkness of evening came on, Mrs Turner began to grow worried, and her son-in-law Francis Bowler went to search for William and Sarah, but without success. On returning home, Bowler was told that his young son had heard the scream of a woman on the moor about 4 pm, but had seen nothing there. The police were informed.

At 9.30 pm Constable Cholerton took a lantern and made a search of the moor, but in the growing dark was unable to find any sign of the missing pair. Cholerton returned to search once again at 4 am on Thursday, 8 May, this time accompanied by Francis Bowler and Mr G Wright. Up on the moor, at a place called Woodbank, the three men stumbled on the corpse of Sarah Carter, covered over with heather. She was no longer a pretty sight, her tongue protruding and her face pale and badly bruised. A mass of bruises on her neck beneath the jaw showed that she had been strangled to death. The dead girl had also been subjected to a sexual assault.

Sickened at this horrible discovery, the searchers had gone only a short way further when they found William Turner. The killer was hanging by a rope from a nearby yew tree, and was also dead. In his pockets Cholerton and the others found Sarah's cap, and a number of stones. As far as could be seen, William Turner had helped the girl to gather a few sticks, and had then seized her, throwing her down on her back to rape and strangle her with his bare hands. The rope, which had been taken to fasten the sticks, Turner had fitted in a noose round his neck, filled his pockets with the stones, climbed the yew and fastened the other end to a branch, and sprung off to his death. A violent, jealous, passionate man, William Turner had been true to his word. Faced with the loss of the girl he loved, knowing his feelings were not returned, he had ensured that 'no one else shall have her'. In the end he had possessed her body, but his triumph – if it can be called that – must have been bitter indeed. In the end, both he and his victim had left the world within minutes of each other, each by a sudden act of terrible violence, through murder and suicide.

The green-eyed monster had struck again.

Chapter 21

A Scandalous Assault
1875

Sarah Lock was only too well known to her neighbours in the village of Whitwell, on the eastern edge of Derbyshire close to the Nottinghamshire border. A rowdy frequenter of local public houses – usually in the company of her husband, John Lock, who worked as a stonemason on the Duke of Portland's estate at Welbeck – she was known for her lively dancing and singing of indecent songs, as well as for exchanging 'near the knuckle' banter with the other drinkers. Sarah could hardly be regarded as an innocent, but nothing in her behaviour called for the violent and shameful treatment she was to undergo on Good Friday, 26 March 1875.

At half-past six that evening John and Sarah entered the *Half Moon,* on Chesterfield Road, Worksop, a mile or so from their home in Whitwell. Both had already been drinking by the time

The village of Whitwell, east Derbyshire, home of the unfortunate Sarah and John Lock. Dennis Middleton

five other regulars arrived at 8 pm. Richard Broom, Samuel Pritchard, and James Burton were all miners, Broom the oldest at thirty-three, while the others were both only twenty-one. The occupations and ages of the other two, John Taylor and Henry Allison, are not divulged. The group ordered ale, and ate some bread and cheese. Half an hour later Charles Presley, a native of Shuttlewood, near Bolsover, came in. Seeing Mrs Lock, he asked her to sing, and Sarah was only too happy to oblige. We are not told exactly what she sang, but it may well have been something of a suggestive nature. At any rate, it was enough for Richard Broom to buy her a glass of whiskey, and coax another song from her. Apparently the landlady, Mary Roberts, disliked Sarah singing in her establishment – no doubt the type of songs in the latter's repertoire had something to do with it – and after an hour or so of this bawdy entertainment she decided that she had heard enough. She spoke to Sarah and her husband, both of whom were fairly well inebriated by now, and the couple left the pub, accompanied by Charles Presley. Mrs Roberts was later to state that the Locks were not fully drunk, but evidently felt concerned enough to ask Presley to see them home. As they made for the door, one of the men in the group told Sarah not to worry as 'we are all going your way home.'

According to Sarah Lock's own recollections, Presley walked with them about a hundred yards along the Old Road, and as they chatted together Richard Broom joined them, and asked her to return to the *Half Moon* for another glass. To this Sarah claimed to have replied that she had already had enough to drink, but Broom was not to be put off. He produced a bottle from his coat, and again tried to persuade them to drink with him. Sarah claimed that she refused, but this was later disputed by Broom.

Soon afterwards the rest of the group caught up with them, remarking on what a pleasant evening it had been, and how they hoped to spend another such in the future. One man reminded her of a song she had sung, entitled 'Down Among the Coals', no doubt alluding to its suggestive lyric, but a second told him that, as miners, they had had enough of being down among the coals all week. After a while it dawned on

Sarah that they were not following the usual route back to her home village, and expressed concern, but one of the group assured her they were all going to Whitwell, and there was no cause for alarm.

They turned the corner down Occupation Road three abreast, with John Lock to Sarah's left and Broom on her right, with the rest of the company close behind. As they reached the gate of a stack yard both Sarah's arms were grabbed and held, by Broom on her right and someone else she couldn't see on her left. Broom, she claimed, then made an indecent proposition to her. He and the others dragged her into the stack yard, and threw her to the ground. Terrified, Sarah yelled for her husband to help her, and Lock tried to push his way to her, but by now the drunken band were ready for him, and he was knocked down in turn. While on the ground he was mercilessly kicked and beaten, and Sarah heard him begging his assailants 'don't murder me quite!' Pinned to the ground, the frightened Sarah had her clothes thrown up, and was brutally 'gang-raped' by the men, two men holding her feet wide apart and a third gripping her head while her attackers took turns. Broom raped her first, then three of the others. She screamed and fought, getting scratched and bruised for her pains, and her husband made further efforts to reach her, but was knocked unconscious.

After they had gone, Sarah – probably still shocked from her ordeal – lay for a time before getting up. She found John Lock lying stunned on the ground with his boots, which had been removed, lying beside him. His pockets had been picked, and although he had lost hardly any money he had been robbed of his hat, a pocket handkerchief and a box key. All their attackers had left was Broom's bottle, which Sarah kept as evidence. The battered couple staggered home, calling en route at the police station, but apparently failed to make anyone hear them. Once they arrived home, at nearly 1 am, Sarah sent their young son to find a policeman. Constable Clifford came in answer to the summons, and saw clear evidence that both had suffered physical violence, and that Sarah had been raped.

The five men were arrested, and appeared at the Summer

The Half Moon, *Chesterfield Road, Worksop, where Sarah was drinking prior to being brutally raped on her way home to Whitwell in 1875.* Dennis Middleton

Assizes at Derby Crown Court on Friday, 16 July, Mr Justice Lindley presiding. Broom, Pritchard, Burton, Allison and Taylor all faced the charge of violently assaulting and ravishing Sarah Lock on 26 March. Sarah appeared and gave her testimony, which was corroborated by her husband. John Lock claimed that he had first been knocked down by Taylor after Broom made the improper suggestion to his wife. Felled a second time, he had seen Pritchard and Burton holding Sarah's feet 'a yard and a half off', while another man held her head, and Broom was 'kneeling upon his wife'. After that he was subjected to a kicking and his boots were dragged off, but before losing consciousness heard someone call out to 'take the bugger his boots back, or we shall be taken up for highway robbery'.

Also called was Charles Presley, together with a local farmer, John Gee. The latter recalled hearing cries between 10 pm and 11 pm, and he and his companion Joseph Pearce went to investigate. They had encountered Allison, who had fallen through a hedge, being picked up by Taylor. Gee asked what they were doing out at this time of night, but got no answer. Going further on, he and Pearce saw other men on the turnpike road, but were unable to identify them.

The defence case was based almost entirely on attempts to discredit the testimony of the Locks. In this respect, Sarah made herself an easy target. On a previous occasion, she had accused a man of assaulting her in Eckington, only to have the case dismissed. Her penchant for drinking and racy behaviour was well known. Joseph Pearce, who had accompanied John Gee in his search on the night of the rape, testified that on Whit Monday Sarah had been in the *Boot and Slipper* public house, where she had changed partners while dancing in a suggestive manner, and later on – the worse for drink – asked Pearce to come outside with her. Pearce had pushed her away from him, only to be accused of trying to take liberties with her. Mary Roberts, the landlady of the *Half Moon*, confirmed that Mrs Lock had been drinking, and had been turned out of the public house for her unseemly behaviour. Broom and his associates implied that she had gone with them willingly, and was not taken advantage of. Sarah hotly denied all these accusations, claiming she had missed her way in the dark, and was not guilty of the actions described by Pearce and Mrs Roberts, but her rebuttals were less than convincing. If the case had depended solely on her own and her husband's account of the events, their attackers might well have been acquitted.

As it was, the prosecution was able to muster more crucial testimony and evidence. Mrs Roberts identified the bottle they produced as 'very like' the ginger beer bottle she had filled with a gill of gin at Richard Broom's request before he left the *Half Moon*. Mr Walker, a surgeon, gave the results of his medical examination of Sarah, which indicated that she had suffered injuries due to sexual assault, and Constable Clifford confirmed that he had found husband and wife with 'traces of the assault which had been committed upon them.' At this point the prosecution withdrew its charge against Henry Allison, presumably because he could not be positively identified as having taken part in the attack. The Judge, Mr Justice Lindley, while summing up, noted that the evidence against John Taylor being directly involved rested on the statement from Mr Lock, who 'believed' that Taylor had knocked him down, and that the jury should bear this in mind. Taylor was duly acquitted of the charge.

The other three were not so lucky. The ring-leader Richard Broom was convicted, together with Samuel Pritchard and John Burton, both of whom had been identified by Lock as having taken part with Broom in the brutal rape of his wife. All three were sentenced to ten years' penal servitude.

For Sarah Lock and her husband, it may have taken longer than that to eradicate the events of that terrible Good Friday night from their minds. If they ever did.

Chapter 22

Found Dead in the River Rother
1875

t was Monday, 12 July 1875, and Charles Webster, having worked his shift at New Whittington colliery, had decided to take the afternoon off. He and his friend Cornelius Warburton were fishing a stretch of the River Rother that lay between Firth's Works and Staveley Railway Station, close to the village of Barrow Hill. All at once, Warburton pointed out a man and woman about fifty yards away from them. The woman was standing, while the man was seated, but as the two afternoon fishermen watched, the man got up and both he and his companion moved off along the footpath towards Barrow Hill until they reached a stile between Marsden's and Pattison's Meadows. At this point the man stopped by the stile while the woman clambered over and disappeared. She did not return for maybe fifteen minutes, and seemed rather agitated. The man had to help her over the stile, and supported her with a hand on the shoulder as she staggered for a moment. Both walked away towards New Whittington, crossing a field before sitting down again at the next stile. Their behaviour struck Webster and Warburton as suspicious, and the latter moved closer, hiding behind a tree to see what they would do next. Eventually they went away, and the two men returned to the riverside to continue their fishing.

Suddenly Warburton called his friend over to the water's edge. Joining him, Webster saw what looked like a parcel wrapped in newspapers, lying by some tree roots near the river. The place where it lay was near the hedge in Pattison's field, seventy-eight yards from the stile that separated Marsden's and Pattison's properties. Picking up the parcel and opening it, Webster was shocked to find that he was holding the corpse of a young child wrapped in two newspapers and 'two pieces of stuff, one black and the other coloured.' Although the outer newspaper was wet, the inner wrapping was still dry, and it was clear that the parcel had not been submerged in the river. Webster quickly set off for Barrow Hill, and showed the body to Constable John Curtis, explaining what he and Warburton had seen. Curtis was also present when a post-mortem examination was carried out the following day by the Chesterfield surgeon Dr John Bluett. Bluett found the corpse, that of a little girl, to be badly decomposed, especially round the head, which showed signs of bruising consistent with its having sustained heavy blows to the skull and scalp. There was no fracture of the skull, but the bones were 'a good deal driven one upon another.' A close examination of the child's lungs revealed that it had lived and breathed, and was unlikely to have met its death by drowning, having been only a short time in the water. Dr Bluett concluded that death had been caused by the blows to its head, before it came near to the Rother, and that the child had been dead for at least three days. Shortly afterwards, following up on the information provided by Webster and his friend, the police arrested a couple of tramps, Joseph Woodward and Eliza Carlisle, who appeared to fit the description of the pair seen by the river. They were brought before the Chesterfield magistrate Bernard Lucas on Tuesday 13 July, the day of the post-mortem, on suspicion of causing the death of a child at Barrow Hill the previous day, and were remanded in custody until Thursday. The next day an inquest was held, at which evidence was heard from Constable Curtis, Charles Webster and the surgeon, John Bluett. The doctor's findings merely added to the mystery surrounding the death of the child. It had at first been assumed that the woman, Eliza Carlisle, had borne an illegitimate baby and decided to dispose of it to avoid the public disgrace. Bluett, however, was able to demonstrate that the child could not possibly be hers. The baby girl had weighed between eight and nine pounds, and it was the view of the surgeon that unless the mother was a large woman, the labour must have been protracted. Bluett had examined Carlisle and was positive she had not borne a child recently, and probably not at all. To clinch matters further, he had discovered that she was now two or three months pregnant! Obviously whoever the mother of the child had been, it was not Eliza Carlisle.

The jury at the inquest returned a verdict 'Found Dead in the River Rother', but Woodward and Carlisle were not yet in the clear. The suspicion now was that they had undertaken to dispose of the unwanted child on behalf of someone else, either for money or for other reasons. As a result, they were brought before Magistrate E G Maynard a few days later, where Charles Webster and Constable Curtis gave evidence. So too did John Lewis, night foreman at Frith & Sons, who had overheard Carlisle talking about seeing a parcel near the river, and questioned her about it. Lewis made a 'citizen's arrest' and accompanied her to the constable's house, going on himself to interrogate Woodward. The latter, hearing Carlisle was now in custody, replied that in that case he 'might as well go'. Both were remanded to await trial.

Then, all at once, everything seems to go quiet. Neither Woodward nor Carlisle appeared at the Assizes to face charges, and they do not seem to have been sentenced to imprisonment. One can only assume that the evidence produced was of such a circumstantial nature that it was impossible to convict them of causing the death, especially as the identity of the child's mother remained a mystery. Perhaps their case was overshadowed by the arrest of Ellen Sawyer, a North Wingfield woman, only a few weeks later, after she confessed to burning her child in the fire. A year earlier she had been suspected of disposing of another child in the river, in a manner remarkably similar to that of the two tramps. Sawyer claimed that when the second child was born she had flung it on to the fire 'not knowing whether it was dead or alive'. She was obviously mentally unstable, and had been confined on a previous occasion. Probably this is why she too made no appearance at the subsequent Assizes. All the same, her story must have shocked those who heard it, coming as it did so soon after the body in the Rother.

Chapter 23

A Girl of Good Character
1875

Hannah Owens, a young girl of twenty, had worked as a domestic servant in Chesterfield ever since the autumn of 1874. She had a good name from her employers, who found her honest, pleasant and hard-working. It would seem that she had everything to look forward to, and all her life before her. Yet on the night of Monday 19 July 1875, for reasons that are still not fully explained, Hannah Owens was to cut her own life short.

The first hint of a problem showed itself between September and October 1874, when Hannah was working for George Boot and his wife at the *Old Angel Inn*, off the Market Place in the centre of town. The Boots had been more than satisfied with her work, and found her to be wholly reliable, until a disturbing incident occurred one Saturday night. As Mrs Boot was speaking to her, Hannah suddenly dropped to the ground. The landlady thought she was suffering from a fit, and was no doubt relieved when the young girl came round, but subsequently Mrs Boot discovered that Hannah had been drinking. Clearly this situation could not continue, and Hannah Owens left of her own accord, presumably jumping before she was pushed!

By the middle of the following year, she was holding down a similar job as cook and waitress at the *Rutland Arms* on Stephenson Place, not far from the parish church. Once again, her employers and fellow servants all found her to be a respectable 'girl of good character', who had never been seen drinking or behaving in an improper manner. Unfortunately, it would seem that Hannah had not shaken off her fondness for the bottle, and had merely learned how to hide her problem from her day-to-day acquaintances. Hannah had come to Chesterfield from the mining village of Clay Cross a few miles

Rutland Arms *(now* The Rutland*), Stephenson Place, where Hannah Owens was found hanged after her drunken night in Chesterfield.* Dennis Middleton

to the south of the town, where her father John Owens was a furnace labourer. There she had been keeping company with a young man named Walker, and it was believed that her parents opposed the relationship. It was also claimed by some that at this time she had attempted suicide by throwing herself from the window of her home when her mother and father refused to let her out to meet the young man. Whatever the truth of this,

Hannah had survived, though at exactly what cost remains open to question.

On Sunday, 18 July 1875, having completed her work at the public house, Hannah set off at 6 pm for an evening out. Three hours later she returned to the *Rutland Arms* to take up her evening duties, apparently perfectly sober. But all was not as it seemed. Ann Hibbert, who lived at Soresby Street and helped her widowed mother take in washing, had been friendly with Hannah Owens for the last five months. According to her testimony, Hannah called on her around 6.15 pm on Sunday night, and the pair went out for a stroll round the Market Place at 8 pm. They had been walking only ten minutes or so when, on Packers Row, Hannah complained that she felt dry, and suggested that they have a drink. They went into the *Royal Oak* in the Shambles off the Market Place, and supped a pint of porter before leaving. Back in Packers Row, they met a young man called John Ladin, and talked for a while with him. Ladin was later to claim that he had known Hannah 'since she was a very young girl', and he may well have seen her as a possible conquest. Ladin persuaded the girls to go with him to the *Red Lion* on Vicar Lane, where they met some other young men of their acquaintance. This group paid for a quart of liquor which was drunk by Ladin and the two young women. The inebriated band went on to the *Rutland Arms*, where Hannah bought rum for Ladin and herself. Ladin and the two girls were later seen stumbling along Broad Pavement towards Saltergate by two police constables, who both noted that Hannah was having trouble staying on her feet, but made no effort to interfere. According to Ann Hibbert, she fell down more than once on the way home.

While in a drunken state, Hannah talked incessantly about Walker and her determination to see him again, in spite of her parents wishes. She told Ann she would 'hang for him' and didn't care if she was killed, but would speak to him again. By this time she was so far gone that there was no question of her going back to the *Rutland Arms,* and instead she stayed the night with Ann Hibbert and another girlfriend, Annie O'Brien, at their house on Soresby Street. Ladin, who had gone with them, left the house around 11 pm.

It was 7 am on Monday, 19 July before Hannah returned to the *Rutland Arms*. Elizabeth Harding, the servant, let her in out of the rain, and was shocked at the sight of her workmate's clothes. Her dress was torn, rucked up around her, and badly stained at the front. She told Elizabeth she had stayed the night with Ann Hibbert. Later, around 9.30 am, Elizabeth was cleaning the dram shop while Hannah was washing in the outhouse. At 10 am Elizabeth went to find her, and to her horror discovered Hannah in the water closet in the yard behind the door. She had tied a length of clothes line to one of the rafters, fitted a noose around her neck, and hanged herself. Alerted by Elizabeth's cries, Charles Short, the manager, came running to investigate. He cut the young girl down, but it was far too late. By the time the doctor arrived, Hannah Owens was already dead.

The incident caused a sensation in the town, as Hannah's employers and work colleagues had always found her sober and respectable. The thought of her reeling drunkenly around Chesterfield in the company of inebriated young men, and talking desperately of forbidden love, was too awful to contemplate. At the adjourned inquest on 29 July, Ladin was most anxious to dissociate himself from what had happened, stating that he had never made any improper suggestions to Hannah, or used violence against her. He went so far as to plead that 'I did not propose to sleep with her or anything of that sort.' Whether or not he was believed, it would have been difficult to prove his guilt. The wrath of the coroner was reserved for the two constables, who were rebuked for not intervening. Mr Busby, clearly very angry at the scandal to the town's good name, accused them of inefficiency and even remarked that he did not see what use the police were. He was told that his remarks would be referred to the Chief Constable, but remained unrepentant. In the end, the jury returned a verdict that Hannah had committed suicide while in 'an unsound state of mind resulting from an excessive use of intoxicating liquors.'

What was it that lay behind a young girl's decision to so brutally end her own life? Had something happened on the pub-crawl round Chesterfield that made her decide it was no longer worth going on? Had she yielded to Ladin while in a drunken state, only to regret it afterwards? Or was it despair that overcame her, knowing her parents would never let her have the young man of her choice? Whatever the reason, her decision was short, and final. That Hannah Owens killed herself is all too clear, but why she did it will probably always remain an unanswered question.

Chapter 24

He Has Been a Bad 'Un
1876

One of Chesterfield's long-vanished yards, Taylor's Place, ran off the south side of Holywell Street, close to its junction with Knifesmithgate. Now overlain by modern streets and shops, in the 1870s it was home to some of the town's poorer residents, and like most of Chesterfield's yards was no stranger to drunkenness, squalor and violence. All the same, no-one could have been prepared for the gruesome events of 4 June 1876, which still rank with the most shocking of Chesterfield crimes.

Robert Gwynn, a journeyman nailmaker, lived at Taylor's Place with his wife Margaret and their three grown-up children. Gwynn was sixty-two years old, his wife six years his senior, and the couple had been married for forty years. The itinerant nature of his job meant he was often away from home for long periods, his recent absences including a fifteen-month stay in Barnsley, but it may be the other members of the family regarded this as a blessing. Robert Gwynn was a heavy drinker even by the standards of his day, and – judging by his children's comments – almost certainly an alcoholic, who suffered from 'the blue devils' on occasion. Most of the money he earned went on drink, and led to quarrels with his wife Margaret, who struggled to eke out a meagre living by hawking lace, cotton and other articles in the Chesterfield area. Gwynn was also a habitually short-tempered, violent man, and was at his most dangerous when in drink. In the early June of 1876, he had been at home for three weeks, working for Mr Simpson of Brampton, but had spent his nights consuming as much beer as he could. This drinking had ended with a continuous drunken binge over the three days up to Wednesday, 4 June, with Gwynn growing daily more violent and aggressive.

Apart from his wife and himself, the house at Taylor's Place was occupied by his unmarried son Thomas, his married daughter Katherine and her husband the pipe-moulder Sylvester Kerwin,

Holywell Street, Chesterfield, where at the long-vanished Taylor's Place, a particularly vicious domestic murder was committed in 1876. Dennis Middleton

and young unmarried daughter Margaret, who worked at Mason's tobacco factory in the Spital district. It seems that it was the sixteen-year-old Margaret who brought matters to a head. While her father was out, she had obtained her brother's permission to go to Sheffield for the day. When Gwynn came in, having visited several hostelries and very much the worse for wear, he noticed she was gone, and when his wife returned from her work in the afternoon a quarrel began. 'You've let your daughter go to Sheffield, haven't you?' he accused, and when Mrs Gwynn replied that it was their son who had given permission, her husband threatened to meet the younger Margaret at the station 'and rip her bloody clothes off her back'. Growing angry in turn, his wife told him that if he did she would get a policeman to lock him up. This triggered another vicious outburst from Gwynn, who told her 'I'll make a football of you' and raised his fist.

Mrs Gwynn fled to the next door neighbour's house for safety, while their daughter Katherine, who had witnessed the argument, managed to calm her father down by offering him money for more beer. According to Katherine, after Mrs Gwynn had left the house to go hawking her wares that evening, Gwynn himself went out and sold off his coat, braces and a shirt, no doubt for more drinking funds. On his return he spoke more fondly to Katherine, kissing her and bidding her farewell. He told her he was going to Liverpool, and from there to Ireland, where he would end his days. He then went to bed in the downstairs room he shared with his wife and Margaret.

Margaret did not return home until after 10 pm, by which time her mother had also come home. Mrs Gwynn was talking to her two daughters and Mrs Laden the next door neighbour when Gwynn came running out. Guessing it was Margaret he aimed to hurt, Mrs Gwynn shouted 'run, Maggie! Run!', and the young girl escaped next door as her mother had done not long before. Another quarrel broke out between the mother and father, which continued in their downstairs bedroom. The five inhabitants of the house had only two rooms for sleeping quarters, a garret and a chamber. The Kerwins and Thomas Gwynn shared a bed in the garret, while Margaret usually slept with her parents in the chamber. On her way to this room, she was asked by her father why she was so late, and when she told him she had been to Sheffield she received the ominous reply 'Wait while morning.' By now, though, Margaret was too tired to worry about her father's threats. Getting into bed beside the couple, she was soon asleep.

She awoke suddenly, around 2.15 am, as her mother seized her arm. The older woman tried to say something to her, but all that Margaret heard was a horrible gurgling noise. Looking at her mother, she saw that Mrs Gwynn was bleeding badly from a wound in her throat, and discovered that her father had gone out of the room. Terrified, Margaret screamed out to her brother and the Kerwins to come and help, that 'father is murdering my mother!' At first the three thought she must be dreaming, and Thomas Gwynn told her to go to sleep, but as Margaret continued screaming they realised the seriousness of the situation. Kerwin lit a candle, and opening the door was met by the sight of the frightened Margaret, her chemise spattered and dripping with blood from her mother's wound. Katherine, who had entered her parents' bedroom found Mrs Gwynn lying dead from a wound in the throat that had almost severed her head from her body, and set off screaming in her turn. Warily, and probably feeling some apprehension themselves, Tom and his brother-in-law went in search of Robert Gwynn. Downstairs inside the house they found 'a great stream of blood' on the floor. Presently, they heard a groaning sound from outside, and left the building, moving along the passage that led to the water-closet in the yard. Meanwhile Katherine went to the house of a neighbour, Mrs Hurst, and stood there screaming until the door was opened.

In the passage Tom and Kerwin were again confronted by the appalling sight of blood on the stones, far more this time than there had been in the house. A trail of bare footprints in the blood showed how Gwynn had run out of the house towards the privy. The two could still hear him moaning. They eventually found him lying close to the privy, wearing only a shirt, with his lower body inside the closet and the rest in the passage. He had cut his own throat before running outside. Tom Gwynn roused the neighbours while Kerwin went for the police. Malachi Laden, their next-door neighbour, and Constable Nicholls hurried to the scene, and brown paper was lit and held under Gwynn's nose to see if he was still alive, but by now the drunken nailmaker had struck his last blow. Laden and Nicholls helped the others to carry the dead man back inside the house, where the policeman found the murder weapon lying on the floor inside the downstairs bedroom. This was an open cut-throat razor, which Tom Gwynn would later identify as his own militia razor, and the blade was covered with blood. It was plain to the unwilling witnesses that Robert Gwynn had given vent to a final murderous rage, killing both himself and his unfortunate wife.

The inquest on both bodies took place at the Municipal Hall at 3 pm on Wednesday afternoon, and lasted until 7 pm in the evening. Most of the time was taken by the statements of the witnesses, all of whom agreed on the sequence of events. The jury had no difficulty in agreeing 'that Robert Gwynn murdered his wife while in a state of temporary insanity from the effects of habitual intoxication', and had killed himself while in a similar state. Thomas Gwynn, giving evidence, made a final damning assessment of his late father, stating that: 'He has done his wife no good for the last fifteen years. He used to spend the biggest part of his wages in drink. He has been very queer with her, and has been a "bad 'un".'

All things considered, one cannot help but agree with him.

Chapter 25

A Disgusting and Villainous Crime
1881

lfred Gough was down on his luck. A few years ago, it had all been so different for him. Following a few months with the Leeds Police Force, he had joined the Army, serving for a full term of twelve years with the 17th Regiment of Foot, most of it being spent in India. For some of that time Gough had been an officer's batman. While he had won no medals or decorations, Alfred Gough had evidently won the respect of his officers and fellow soldiers, and was noted for his good conduct. The trouble had started once he left the Army, and returned to England. His money had run out, and Gough had been reduced to a variety of demeaning tasks in order to survive. Two years before, in Sheffield, he had been forced to beg on the streets for money to buy food. Now he had moved to Chesterfield, where he frequented the seedy lodging houses on Church Lane and Lordsmill Street, earning a meagre living as a hawker of toys and novelties in return for rags and bones.

Tall, pock-marked and stooping, with a wispy reddish-brown beard, Gough was a rather unprepossessing figure. All the same, the ex-soldier pushing his handcart had become a familiar sight to many people in the neighbouring villages, especially the young children, who often bought the cheap toys he carried. It had been a long way down from his days in the 17th Foot, and to Gough it must have seemed that he had reached rock bottom. But it was to get far worse, and here Gough himself bore the seeds of his own destruction. It would seem that Alfred Gough harboured darker, forbidden needs that, once unleashed, could only end in tragedy.

On the morning of Saturday 20 August, Gough left Chesterfield and was seen pushing his cart towards the village of Brimington which bordered the town on its north-eastern

Almond Place, Chesterfield Road, Brimington, home of murder victim Eleanor Windle. Dennis Middleton

side. On his way there, at the foot of the hill that led up towards the village along Chesterfield Road, he was met by a group of young girls who were out blackberrying. The toys Gough was selling included a number of small parasols made from pieces of coloured wallpaper, and six-year-old Eleanor Windle took a fancy to one of these. She lived not far away, in a row of houses known as Almond Place, off Chesterfield Road on the far side from the cemetery, and offered to go home and get a halfpenny to buy the toy. She and Gough left the rest of the group and moved away. They did not go immediately to Almond Place. Instead, Gough led the child along a narrow track opposite the cemetery, barely 300 yards from Eleanor's home. This pathway, which was really an access route to Oak House, was known as Johnson's Lane from the brother and sister of that name who lived there.

Shortly afterwards Miss Harriett Johnson, a retired schoolmistress, was outside Oak House and saw Gough and the girl together near the end of the lane. To the horror of the elderly lady, she saw that the hawker had undone his trousers and was exposing himself to the child, who stood innocently watching him. Shocked and angry, Miss Johnson rushed into the house to grab a broom as a weapon, and ran back out and down the lane. She caught sight of them again, but by now Gough had seen her and had no trouble outrunning the older lady. Shepherding Eleanor in front of him, he made off, and by the time Miss Johnson reached the spot, both man and child had disappeared. Miss Johnson looked for them, but without success, and returned to Oak House. She did not report the incident, later remarking rather acidly under questioning that such things were 'far from uncommon' on Johnson's Lane. All the same, it was a pity she did not inform the police, for Miss Johnson was the last person to see Eleanor Windle alive.

Eleanor and her friends often played out, and it was not until around 1 pm, two hours and more after the Johnson's Lane incident, that the child was missed by her parents. By then her father William Windle, had come home from his work as a foreman at Staveley Old Works, and he and his wife grew anxious at their daughter's absence. The alarm was raised, the town crier was sent round the village to rouse the inhabitants, and a search was made of the area. The police were notified, who made a further search, but no sign was found of the missing girl.

Gough, meanwhile, had been seen, without the child, by other witnesses. Around 11.30 am, Sarah Cantrell, wife of a furnace labourer, passed Johnson's Lane on her way to Chesterfield and saw him loading something on to the cart 'which appeared quite full.' At 12.15 pm Elizabeth Neal met Gough en-route to Brimington Common, and exchanged some rags for a parasol for her little girl. She noticed a bundle in the middle of the cart, covered in black cloth, and 'about a quarter stone in weight', but could not make out what it was. Some time after 1.20 pm Mrs Neal saw the hawker again, between her own house and the *Prince of Wales* public house. This time Gough did not stop to chat; he had taken off his coat, and was pushing the cart very quickly, as if in a hurry to get somewhere. Later, but before 2 pm, Sarah Ann Thorley saw Alfred Gough pushing his handcart along the private road from Ringwood towards Barrow Hill. This road is probably the modern Private Drive, Hollingwood, and lies on the far side of Brimington, towards Staveley. Mrs Thorley lived in the lodge at the end of the road, and had a good view of Gough. She noticed that the cart seemed to be heavy, and he was struggling to push it along.

It was 6 pm when Alfred Gough returned to Brimington, halting his cart at the toll-bar house to obtain a glass of ginger beer from the keeper, the splendidly named Charles Abney Hastings Brown. Brown's son was in the Army, and Gough admired the portrait of the young man in his uniform, telling the father of his own service in India. Brown had seen him previously at 9.30 am that morning, coming into Brimington

Private Drive, Hollingwood, where Alfred Gough was seen pushing his handcart, which held the concealed corpse of the murdered child. Dennis Middleton

with his wares. While Gough was at the toll house, he was met by Eleanor's father William Windle, and later by PC Wright, both of whom questioned him as to the child's whereabouts. Windle was not satisfied with some of Gough's evasive answers, and became angry with him. Gough at first appeared not to remember who the child was, and when pressed further, claimed he had only seen her by Windle's house, and that she had walked up the road as if going home. Seeing Windle's evident concern, he asked the father 'is it your girl?', and on being told this was so, remarked that 'it has been a bad job.' As Windle and the constable had not yet obtained the information from Miss Johnson and other witnesses, they were unable to prevent Gough from going back to Chesterfield, where he left his handcart at Thomas Newbury's premises in Brampton and returned to bed down at Spowage's lodging house on Church Lane. Later, around 8 pm, Windle and the constable explored Johnson's Lane, and discovered a space near one of the hedgerows where foxgloves and other plants had been crushed down to a length of four feet, as though someone had sat or lain there. Overnight the search continued, and ponds were dragged, but still the missing child could not be found.

On Sunday 21 August, about 7 am, the toll-keeper Charles Brown decided to search for the little girl himself. He set off down the road to Staveley, and learned that Gough had been seen wheeling his cart along the private Hollingwood Road the previous day. Brown went on as far as Troughbrook Hill, just short of Staveley, and searched the hedgerows beside the road leading off from Inkersall. After a while he returned to the private Hollingwood Road, and eventually reached a wooded area called Hoole's Plantation. Here he found the wheel-marks of a handcart close to the hedge, which indicated that the cart had been manoeuvred sideways to get nearer to the hedge itself. Brown climbed over the railings that bounded the plantation, and followed a path leading through the trees. Almost immediately, he noticed a small bag lying on the ground, and put it into his pocket. Exploring the path to the far end of the plantation, Brown was coming back by another route when he caught sight of a body lying a short way down from the path under a small tree beside an old spoil bank. Scrambling down through the undergrowth, he found the body of a young girl lying on her back, one leg drawn up and her head turned slightly to the left. A hat lay beside her. Brown saw the child was dead, the corpse stiff and cold. Her face and eyes were swollen and discoloured, the reason being a length of sacking which had been wound twice around her neck with such force that the neck was swollen over it. He had found Eleanor Windle.

A man called Edward Tulley was passing by, and Brown called him over and showed him the body. They covered the child up, and on making their way back to the road Brown glimpsed a piece of coloured wallpaper such as Gough used for his toy parasols. This he picked up and took with him, and reported his discovery to the police. Now the hunt was on for Alfred Gough. Superintendent Carline, pursuing enquiries in Chesterfield, found that the hawker had dealings with a shopkeeper in Cavendish Street, and obtained a good description of the wanted man from the manager, Mr J Oliver. Carline's investigations led him to the *Buck Inn* on Holywell Street, where he found Gough drinking alone. The hawker admitted having been in Brimington the previous day, but denied all knowledge of meeting any children. Carline promptly told him he was under arrest, handcuffed him and took him to the station on Marsden Street. The handcart, found on Newbury's premises, was brought to the station soon after.

Gough appeared before the Chesterfield magistrates on Monday morning. The violent death of an innocent child had caused an uproar, and a large crowd assembled outside the offices of Messrs Shipton & Halliwell, solicitors, of West Bars, where the hearing was held. Evidence was heard from Harriett Johnson, Sarah Ann Thorley, and Charles Brown, who had discovered the body. As the handcuffed prisoner was escorted outside, he was met by groans and hisses from the angry crowd, which now filled the courtyard and spilled on to the road. A police cordon was needed to hold them off as Gough was pushed into a cab, which then drove off so hurriedly that a young boy, John Molloy, was knocked down and slightly hurt as

Red Lion Inn, *Brimington, scene of the inquest on Eleanor Windle.* Dennis Middleton

it went through the hostile crowd.

The inquest was held the same afternoon, the jury being sworn at the *Red Lion Inn* in Brimington before going on to view the body at the Windle home at Almond Place. This time William Windle, who had only just seen his dead child, described his actions of the previous day, including his encounter with Gough at the toll-house. The surgeon, Dr William Abraham Walker, reported the findings of his post-mortem. He confirmed that Eleanor Windle had died as a result of strangulation, during which great pressure had been

Brimington Cemetery, Chesterfield Road, where Eleanor was laid to rest following her murder by hawker Alfred Gough. Dennis Middleton

exerted, as the child's neck was 'very much narrowed.' He also revealed that, while he was not positive that Eleanor had been raped, she had certainly undergone a violent sexual assault of some kind before being murdered. Brown repeated his story of the discovery of the body. The inquest was adjourned and resumed the following Friday.

Before then, on Tuesday, William Windle identified Gough at the police station. Obviously distressed at the loss of his child, Windle had fainted when being told the news of her death, and was only with difficulty prevented from attacking Gough during the identification. Eleanor's funeral took place at Brimington Cemetery at 5 pm that afternoon, where the family, accompanied by teachers and schoolfriends, followed the coffin to the grave, and several wreaths were laid. In spite of heavy rain, a huge crowd of people stood outside the cemetery gates to watch the ceremony.

Superintendent Carline had already remarked on the mass of circumstantial evidence to be got through, and added that more witnesses were coming forward every day. Several of these were to testify when the inquest resumed on Friday. The *Red Lion* was to have been the venue, but fearing crowd trouble of the kind they had already encountered at West Bars, the authorities switched the hearing to the Municipal Hall in Chesterfield. In addition to the repeated statements of the earlier witnesses, evidence was heard from Eleanor's playmates, her brother Ernest, and several others. Between them they confirmed Gough's presence in Johnson's Lane with Eleanor at the time of the murder, the fact that he was seen afterwards in Brimington with an unusually heavy cart containing the bag with its mysterious contents, and his journey along the road to Hoole's Plantation where his cart-tracks were found close to the body. These, and the incriminating sack and parasol found by Brown at the scene, were more than enough for the jurors. Incredible as it seemed, there was now surely little doubt that Alfred Gough had committed the assault on his child victim near the hedge in Johnson's Lane, and after strangling her had carried the body through Brimington on his cart – meeting several people on the way – to its eventual resting-place in the wood. To make matters worse, a fellow-inmate of Spowage's lodging house turned up to testify against him. Thomas Holmes, known as 'Mansfield Tom', was a drover, and claimed to have met Gough on his way back from Brimington on Saturday evening. According to Holmes, Gough had informed him that they would not meet again, as 'I have done wrong, and I shall never be happy any more.' Gough made a furious denial, threatening Holmes with violence, and whether he did in fact make such a confession remains open to question.

Certainly it did nothing to help his case. The jury returned a verdict of wilful murder, and Gough was held in custody until he was due to appear before a higher court. Alfred Gough came before the Grand Jury at Leicester in November 1881, where the evidence was heard, and the same verdict reached. Convicted of what was described as 'a disgusting and villainous crime', he was hanged at Leicester prison on 21 November.

His actions on that fateful day in August strongly suggest that Gough harboured paedophile tendencies, and the question naturally arises as to whether this was the only time they had mastered him. Had he somehow managed to suppress these dark desires during his time in the Army? Or had he indulged them in secret while in India, and escaped detection? It is unlikely we shall ever know. One suspects that by 1881 Alfred Gough had already entered his own kind of hell. It is all the more tragic that, in the course of his downfall, he also claimed the life of an innocent child.

Chapter 26

You Have Kicked Me to Death
1882

In Chesterfield in the 1880s, violence was an everyday fact of life. Nor was it confined to the centre of town. While the dimly-lit yards off the Market Place remained notorious for brawls, muggings and the activities of prostitutes, things were not so very different on the other side of town. The *Rutland Arms*, almost within touching distance of the parish church, had already seen the tragic suicide of Hannah Owens. In 1882 it was the setting for a vicious scuffle which saw George Coles die after being felled by an ugly, drunken prize-fighter called Flint. Five years later, in 1887, a similar unseemly brawl some fifty yards away in Tapton Lane would result in another death.

Drink, too, was to fuel the savage event that took place just across the road from the church, in Station Lane, on Saturday 28 January 1882. Station Lane, the modern Station Road, was a row of houses running off from behind Corporation Street to the *Derbyshire Times* offices and the junction with Station Back Lane. In 1882 Dennis Gorman was in his fourth year as Librarian at the Stephenson Memorial Hall on Corporation Street. In his time he had encountered murderers and desperate men, but one suspects that he would have been appalled had he known what was about to happen so close to his place of work.

William Goddard and his wife Sarah were recent arrivals from Sheffield, and had been at No 5 Station Lane for only three days, having previously lived on Victoria Street. In the short time they had known her, Mrs Goddard's neighbours found her to be a quiet and pleasantly spoken person. William Goddard, who worked as a journeyman slater for Mr Reuben Wragg, made quite a different impression. Addicted to strong drink, he was frequently the worse for wear, and had several times been heard engaging in loud arguments with his wife on returning from the local hostelries. It was later to emerge that although the couple

Station Road, Chesterfield. As Station Lane, in 1882, it was to be the scene of the terrible 'Chesterfield kicking case' murder. Dennis Middleton

had been married for fourteen years and had four children, theirs had been a stormy relationship, and at one point they had separated for eighteen months, due to Goddard's violence and heavy drinking. A thick-set, powerful man, lacking one eye, with 'a rather intelligent but unquestionably pugilistic appearance', he was not one to be crossed when in his cups. Mrs Goddard, slight and frailly built, was evidently afraid of him. And, as events were to prove, she had every right to be.

It was half past eleven on Saturday night, 28 January 1882, and at No 3 Station Lane Mrs Hannah Sharman was preparing supper for her collier husband, who was due to return from his shift. All at once she heard a fearful scream from the direction of No 5, a couple of doors away. As she listened, a second scream rang out. Mrs Sharman hurried into the yard, and saw the door of No 5 was open. Then she saw Mrs Goddard moving slowly up the yard towards her, obviously hurt and in great pain. She asked Mrs Sharman to take hold of her, and the other woman shepherded her gently inside the house. On being asked what was the matter, Mrs Goddard begged her would-be rescuer to protect her, as: 'my husband has kicked me, and I am bleeding to death.'

Looking down, Mrs Sharman was horrified to see that her neighbour was indeed bleeding very badly from beneath her clothes and on to the ground, with blood running down the door steps and along the yard. Once inside, Sarah Goddard swayed as if about to faint, and fell to her knees. Mrs Sharman offered the injured woman a chair, only for Mrs Goddard to reply that she could not sit down.

Realising that her neighbour was badly hurt, Hannah Sharman called for help from Mrs Worrall, who came to the house. Shocked by the blood all over the floor, she too heard the victim's story of what had been done to her. Mrs Worrall set off for the Goddard house, and called out for Sarah's husband. William Goddard did not appear at once, and it was later surmised that he was trying to hide himself upstairs. After repeated calls he came outside, to be berated by Mrs Worrall who on hearing his claim that he had not harmed his wife told him shortly: 'you villain, you have – you've murdered her!' Goddard continued to protest his innocence, but went with her to the Sharman house, where the injured woman now leaned helplessly against the wall of the kitchen, growing weak from loss of blood. Goddard came in, and tugged at the dress of his wife, speaking gently to her as 'Sally' and 'Sarah, my lass', and asking her to come home with him. She answered feebly: 'Oh, Bill, I can't walk. You have kicked me to death.' Angry and disgusted at his affected kindness after what had been done, Hannah Sharman firmly forbade him to move Sarah from the house.

By this time a third neighbour, Elizabeth Bashforth, had joined the group. She lived at No 6 next to the Goddards, and had seen William come home earlier on. The jury were later to learn that he had been drinking for three hours at the *Free Trade Hotel* at Saltergate. Like the other two women, Mrs Bashforth had heard the screams, and the noise of someone running up the stairs. Now she too confronted him and accused him of having injured his wife. Not satisfied with his claim that he 'had never touched her', Mrs Bashforth went in search of a policeman.

Goddard left the house, and was seen running along the passage, evidently intending to make his escape. Panic, and the drink he had taken, acted against him, and he seems to have gone aimlessly to the Midland railway station only to turn back and up nearby Tapton Lane. Unfortunately for him, his wayward escape route would only take him into the arms of the law. Mrs Bashforth had found P C George Dolphin, who was patrolling in Holywell Street, and at her request the constable accompanied her to the Sharman house. There he found Sarah Goddard lying in a pool of blood just inside the door. Seeing that she was close to death, Dolphin left the house to find a doctor, and on the way met Goddard coming up near the top of Tapton Lane. Dolphin had been given a description of him, and immediately collared him, accusing him of the violent attack, which Goddard again denied. The two of them went to fetch the surgeon Dr John Bluett, who returned with them to the Sharman house.

On arriving there, between midnight and 1 am, Bluett saw at once that there was little to be done. Sarah Goddard lay on her back, still bleeding slightly, but with virtually no pulse, and unable to speak or respond in any way to his queries. Blood stained the floor all the way from the door to where she lay. Lifting her clothes, the surgeon found 'an immense quantity of clotted blood'. This was cleared away by the women 'in double handfuls', and Elizabeth Bashforth was later to confess to being sickened by

Tapton Lane, where fugitive William Goddard was arrested by PC George Dolphin.
Dennis Middleton

what she had witnessed. On Bluett's instructions, the injured woman was given a stimulant and placed by the fire, and after staying with her another hour the surgeon left. Soon afterwards he returned, only to be told that Sarah Goddard was now dead. Earlier on, while the poor woman was still breathing, Bluett had demanded of Goddard 'how he could have illused her so brutally', to which the husband made his customary protestations of innocence. To this, the good doctor responded that 'she has been brutally treated by somebody, and she will certainly die.' It had not taken long for his prophecy to be fulfilled. Bluett's post-mortem soon afterwards revealed massive bruising of the groin, and severe injury to the vagina, consistent with a violent blow. In the surgeon's opinion, this would have ruptured the blood vessels, causing the fatal haemorrhage. It might have been caused by Mrs Goddard falling on to a chair or a table edge, but he thought it unlikely. Rather, Bluett felt that the wretched woman had died as the result of a vicious kicking; hob-nailed boots such as those worn by William Goddard would have caused such an injury, and he judged that three blows had been delivered. The other possibility put forward, that the injuries had been caused by falling against a chair or table, or by falling down the stairs, he regarded as most unlikely.

The following Monday William Goddard appeared before a coroner's jury, when statements were given by Hannah and Abraham Sharman, Elizabeth Bashforth, PC Dolphin and Dr Bluett. The surgeon praised the Sharmans for doing all they could for the dying woman, and repeated his opinion that Sarah Goddard had died as the result of a kick from the toe of a boot. While in custody, Goddard had claimed that when he returned home on Saturday night expecting his dinner, his wife had presented him with a candle, and told him to 'take thy clothes and go'. This appeared to have roused a certain amount of sympathy with some of the male jury – a sympathy noticeably absent from the testimony of the female witnesses – and a verdict of manslaughter was returned, Goddard being committed for trial at the next Assizes on the lesser charge. Incredibly, at the end of the inquest the prisoner was greeted by a juryman, grocer Frank Harrison, who shook hands with him and remarked: 'I am very sorry for you, Bill, my boy, but I stuck to you back and edge.' Luckily for Mr Harrison his action was not noticed until he had left, as otherwise he would have been fined for contempt. Apparently another juryman later boasted that he was glad to have saved a man from hanging.

These, and other aspects of the case, led the Public Prosecutor to call for Goddard to return to face prosecution on the Thursday of the same week. This time a verdict of wilful murder was returned, and he was committed to the Assizes on a capital charge. These took place at Derby on Thursday 9 February, and after hearing all the evidence the jury came back with a verdict of manslaughter. Significantly, the judge's summing up, which lasted an hour, was reported to be 'almost entirely against the prisoner'. Sentence was deferred until the following day, and Goddard, who had hitherto shown no emotion, wept as he left the dock. When Mr Justice Hawkins finally passed sentence, he confessed that 'I can find no circumstances of palliation in your case; it is a crime closely approaching to murder.' In his opinion, the only thing that prevented him from sentencing Goddard to life imprisonment was the lack of any evidence of previous cruelty to his wife. All the same, he informed the prisoner that he was guilty of 'an act of as sheer brutality as any man can be guilty of', and awarded the maximum sentence it was in his power to give. William Goddard was sentenced to twenty years penal servitude.

Coming as it did only a few months after Gough's murder of Eleanor Windle, the 'Chesterfield Kicking Case', as it was called, shocked the whole town. It bears some disturbing similarities to the Bennett case of 1872, where another woman died in virtually identical circumstances. The only real difference was that in Bennett's case, the luckless wife was the alcoholic. In 1882, William Goddard was both drunkard and murderer. Perhaps most disturbing of all, the jury's verdict was the same for both men. Like Bennett, Goddard was responsible for a savage killing, and escaped the gallows. One suspects that, had the jury been made up of some of the female witnesses, he would not have been so lucky.

Two decades inside a Victorian prison would have been no picnic, but William was luckier than his unfortunate wife. No doubt Hannah Sharman and her friends felt that, when it came to justice, it was still very much a man's world.

Index